HOLOCAUST GIRLS

HOLOCAUST GIRLS

S.L. WISENBERG

History, Memory
& Other Obsessions

University of Nebraska Press
Lincoln & London

All photographs courtesy of the author.

Acknowledgments for use of previously published material appear on pages 141–42, which constitute an extension of the copyright page.

© 2002 by the University of Nebraska Press
All rights reserved
Manufactured in the United States of America

∞

ISBN 0-8032-4801-6

LOC control number:
2001052672

IN MEMORIAM

Jesse A. Silesky
(1987–2001)
AND
Avrohm I. Wisenberg
(1920–1991)

CONTENTS

Illustrations

Acknowledgments

I would like to thank the Ragdale Foundation, Millay Colony for the Arts, Fine Arts Work Center in Provincetown, Illinois Arts Council, and National Endowment for the Humanities for fellowships and stipends.

I am indebted to Dan Sharon the Wonder Librarian and staff at the Asher Library at the Spertus Institute of Jewish Studies in Chicago, research assistants provided by Northwestern University's Medill School of Journalism and the Women's Residential College, as well as the staff of the *Centre de Documentation Juive Contemporaine* in Paris. Northwestern's Gender Studies Program supported me as a visiting scholar, giving me access to the library and other university resources.

I would also like to thank the many people over the years who have offered encouragement, support, information, and wisdom:

The Writer Gals, past and present: Pamela Erbe, Garnett Kilberg Cohen, Tsivia Cohen, Catherine Scherer, the late Julie Showalter, Janice Rosenberg, Terri Mathes, Joyce Winer, Peggy Shinner, Sharon Solwitz, Carol Levenson, Fran Zell

The Biographers' Support Group: Fran Paden, Carolyn De Swarte Gifford, Marguerite De Huszar Allen

Scholars: Anton Kaes, the late James E. B. Breslin, the ever-patient Anita Turtletaub

Traveling companions and hosts: Angie Cannon, Lara Dämmig, Jeff Segall, Jessica Jacoby, Stefan Cziep, Ellen Witman, Carol Bodenheimer, Judith Katz, and Debbie Long

Writers, readers, editors, and friends who have helped and inspired both directly and indirectly: Barry Silesky, Dan Howell, Seth and the late Jesse Silesky, Jennifer Berman, Jack Doppelt, Don Wiener, Anne Redlich, Rosellen Brown, Robin Hemley, Phil Berger, Mitch Newman, Alison True, Pat Arden, Paula Kamen, Yuliya Ratner, Ben Evans, Bill Stamets, Dinah Wisenberg Brin, Otto Schlamme, Sharon Brener, Rick Soll, Jim Winters, Jessica Seigel, Valerie Denney, Christina Villaseñor, the staff at Café Avanti, Chuck Burack, Linc Cohen (*compagnon extraordinaire*), Rosi Wisenberg Fink, and Evelyn Wisenberg.

Der Got fun mayn umgloybn iz prekhtik.
[Great is the God of my disbelief.]

Jacob Glatstein, "Mayn Vog'l Bruder" ("My Fellow-Wanderer")

HOLOCAUST GIRLS

HOLOCAUST GIRLS/LEMON

We are the Holocaust Girls
The Holocaust Girls, the Holocaust Girls
We are the Holocaust Girls,
We like to dig in the dark.

to the tune of "Lullaby League and
Lollypop Guild" from *The Wizard of Oz*

1.

You don't have to be Jewish to be a Holocaust Girl. But it helps. It
helps to have been born in the U.S.A. to parents born here, without
accents. But it's not necessary. And you don't have to be a girl, either.
What matters most is that you must love suffering. You have to pick
at wounds, must be encumbered by what you consider an affliction.
You have to see your pain as a dark hole you could fall into. You practice falling into the darkness. You immerse yourself in descriptions of
horror. You stand in the library aisle in the World War II–Europe section and thumb through familiar pages. You stare at the photographs
of the skeletons, compositions you've memorized. You watch your
tears make little dents, like tiny upturned rose petals, on the pages.

2.

Sometimes, what you have to do is jump.

In Lvov, Poland, which was also known as Lemberg, and which
became L'viv, Ukraine, the Jews were trapped with no place to go. It
was 1943, the time of daily roundups and shootings. *Aktions*. The
Jews of the town were cornered. There was no escape, only the possibility of hiding, disappearing. A number of daring, desperate souls
stepped down into the sewers and lived there. Eleven of them survived, among the rats and slime and damp, without sun, for fourteen
months. They paid jewelry and gold and devalued zlotys to the sewer
workers who found them and kept them alive. When the Germans re-

treated, when the Russians reclaimed the city, the Jews emerged from the sewer. They were pale as larvae. Covered in filth, backs hunched. Dripping. Their pupils had shrunk, too small to hold daylight. Everything looked blood red to them, or black and white. A crowd formed and stared at them; they seemed like cavemen. The group found its way to an empty apartment, climbed the stairs. The young mother among them, Paulina Chiger, took her two children to a window and opened it. "Breathe the air," she told them; they breathed, looking down at the street through a blood-red haze. "Breathe deeply the fresh air."

The Aryan side of Warsaw, it has been said, looked the same as it always had except there were no Jews. The ghetto revolt began in April 1943. In early May, before the ghetto burned completely, after particularly wrenching battles, a Jewish resistance fighter named Tuvia Borzykowski, along with seven of his comrades, slipped down to the sewers to pass to the Aryan side. It was dangerous; all day the Germans had been sending gas and grenades into the sewers. After walking and crawling underground for several hours, the eight men saw a huge light. It could only be Germans looking for Jews. Borzykowski and his friends froze, resigned to discovery and death.

But instead: two friends and a sewer worker, looking for survivors of the revolt. They carried candy and lemons. Borzykowski took a lemon. "It was the first fresh food we had tasted in months," he remembered. He bit into the lemon, ate it, peel and all.

That is what the Holocaust Girls yearn for – to want and appreciate something as intently, as specifically, as that whole lemon, to love the air and sun as much as the family crouched fourteen months in the sewers of Lvov.

They want to greet lovers with that lemon, night after night. They want to see the dark hunger, the preternatural need. They want to *be* that lemon, consumed by one survivor after the other.

That they can't explain this to anyone is part of their tragedy.

3.

The Holocaust Girls want to haunt people, from far away, from another childhood. They want everyone to know they have unreachable souls. They want people to understand that their beings can't be easily grasped or understood, the way it's hard to make the link between the half-century-old photo of prisoners in a bunk, the face of young Elie Wiesel circled, and the glossy photo of the now–Nobel Laureate. It's hard to make the cognitive leap from the one stick among other sticks to the American man in a suit, wearing matching socks, silk or otherwise tie, shoes with names, perhaps (wing tips, oxfords), his hair cut professionally – in short, civilized. In short, named.

4.

Whenever the Holocaust Girls have a task to do, when they're standing in the 15-items-or-fewer line at the supermarket, and the other customers are looking at *People* or turning the pages of the *Weekly World News*, the Girls are looking deep into the darkness of Liz Taylor's newsprint eyes, they're imagining roll call, when prisoners in the camps lined up – 15 degrees, wooden clogs, thin filthy clothing, empty stomachs – standing hour upon hour. They're wondering if they would have collapsed. They're wondering if they would have formed alliances with strangers with similarly shaven heads, if anyone would have loved them hard enough or loved life fiercely enough to have saved them crusts of bread and slipped them filched potatoes. "Do you have a preferred card?" asks the young cashier at the Jewel, and the person in front of the Holocaust Girl hands over her card. The Girl waits, sighing, while the cashier summons an older employee to ring up the six-pack of beer. The Girl always finds it odd that teenagers aren't allowed to push the register buttons for liquor, but the Girl feels strangely reassured in the shelter of letter-of-the-law rules. A few minutes later she's trudging down the street, one plastic bag dangling from each arm, on her way home. Home, home, says the Holocaust Girl under her breath. She knows how lucky she is to have always had a home, keys, heat. She looks at her wooden floors and doesn't allow herself to wish for a big rug, Oriental, magenta with a golden mandala-like design, flamboyantly fringed, deep pile. *Comfort*, it would sing to her, *comfort*.

SHEMA, THE FIRST PRAYER
YOU LEARN

It begins in bed. Before sleepiness. "Repeat after me," says your father. "It goes like this: *Shema Yisra'el adonay eloheynu adonay echad.*" You learn the English alongside, without punctuation: "Hero Israel the Lord are God the Lord is one." You don't think about what it means. Later you learn it's "Hear, O Israel: The Lord our God . . ." And later you learn the next line, less familiar, and therefore more special, serious: *Baruch shaym kevod* . . . , after which you begin the list in English, as a kind of translation: "God bless Mommy/ Daddy/Rosi/Greg the Dachshund/Grandma Bessie/Grandma Dallas and Pa . . ." The sleek black dog is in between the older sister and the in-town grandmother, which is where he stands in your affections. Where he belongs. He belongs outside, says your mother. Greg is an outside dog. You pray for him to be let inside.

The Shema, the first prayer you learn. A sign that the day has ended. Giving over to it. Separation of light and dark. The noise and the quiet. The door is closed.

As you grow older, you learn that the Shema has been written down. You learn other prayers, but the Shema keeps its status as the first, fundamental. It is not frilly, like its companion prayer Ve'ahavta further down the page in the prayer book. The Ve'ahavta is coquettish, with its rhyming, wending *echa* suffixes: *elohecha, levavecha, me'odecha*. This is the fancy stuff, more dazzling, almost prissy, or at least that's the way the Bat Mitzvah girls sing it. When the cantor chants it at services, his strong slow voice re-ennobles it. But the Ve'ahavta does not sound like a prayer for the end of the day. It is not yet familiar enough.

In Hebrew school, you learn a joke. A dark adult joke, different from the plays on words that the boys in the back of the class make. They sing, for example, "Elvin Hayes" instead of "Ayl b'nai" during the Passover song "Adir Hu." And they say "Minnie Horowitz" instead of "min ha'aretz" – from the earth – during the prayer over the bread. This is the joke, told by the Hebrew teacher who speaks English with an accent: "In the ancient times, the time of domination, the Jew with no money takes a job as the lion in the Colosseum. There is a fifty percent chance he will die from it. On all fours, deep inside of his hot, close costume, he sees the real lion charge at him. The Jew begins the Shema, the prayer of faith you will die with on your lips. He reconciles himself to this dance with death, this chance of death, because otherwise he and his family will die. Because they will starve. He cannot provide. He takes a breath, open to the jaws of death. He hears the other lion who finishes his prayer."

Both are imposters, it turns out. Impoverished Jews. Mere men. The joke ends there. The teacher then turns to the serious stuff. Hebrew grammar. Biblical kings. Does not continue, does not explain what the crowd, deprived of its daily or weekly bloodlust, will do. Will the mob kill both of the men?

Or do the men engage in a to-the-death struggle, each to kill his own, amid the cheers of the crowd, which does or does not understand what it is watching?

This is not a before-bedtime joke. It is an off-center joke, the way everything the Hebrew teacher does is hopelessly foreign, like the way she drew beards and mustaches on the boys' faces for the Purim play, using permanent markers instead of eyebrow pencil. This is like a wayward April Fool's prank, like when you told your mother there was a bee in the bedroom, and then five minutes later – saw a real bee fly in. It is like a frog put in a cigar box as a surprise and then forgotten as he suffocates in the tobacco-moist confines. The story of the lion brothers comes back to you at night.

Hero Israel. The Lord is one. Abraham smashed the idols in his father's idol shop (something like a sculpture gallery, you always imagined) and God said, "Good," and Abraham said, "Fine," and "We will worship just one," and shaped some prayers just for Him.

You are in bed alone with the Shema, the first prayer you learned, the one your mother and father say to each other at night. In good faith. When you're older you'll learn to lilt your voice for Ve'ahavta like the other Bat Mitzvah girls, orchids pinned to velvets and moires. Later you'll read that, when praying alone, you should add, "God, faithful king!" You never do this. Later you will understand the translation: "And these words which I command thee this day, shall be upon thine heart. Thou shalt teach them diligently unto thy children. . . ." Later you will be faced with lions, wandering/wanting/ hoping they are Jews underneath – soul mates – who know the ends to your prayers.

By then you will have absorbed some history and culture, enough to know that the lion story is the quintessential Jewish joke, which traditionally involves smart, weak people in impossible situations. They have only words to save themselves. In this case, the words of the joke, in future tellings.

The Jew speaks, so that the future will hear it.

The Jew prays, using words that ancestors knew that their ancestors knew.

By the time you get to graduate school, much of your life is spent with Quakers and other pacifists, planning rallies and protests. You're an atheist, you think, but a Jewish atheist, and you know that there's even a tradition of nonbelievers. Still, on Friday nights you have dinner with three Jewish friends and you light candles and drink wine and break bread, reciting the blessings. You discuss poetry and heritage. How do you explain it? A tidal pull.

At formal services, which you attend erratically, you say the Shema along with everyone else. Sometimes you're provided with a Hebrew term for the female aspect of God. The prayer is as familiar to you as your pulse. You welcome it, an old friend: Oh, you, still around, after all these years?

Each time you come home it's a surprise anew that your parents still recite the Shema, each to each, witnesses, pajamas and cold cream and hot pad, and they are surprised that you have stopped something as natural and necessary as brushing your teeth.

All this time, they've recited it, without question, a matter of faith combined with habit, decided long ago.

And you try but you can't remember when you stopped saying the Shema. And it's not their faith that you envy so much as their daily acceptance of the mystery of oneness – the oneness of unbroken repetition, the chain they are still a part of.

KAVKA/40

1. KAFKA, THE JEW I USED TO BE

I used to think there was only one Kafka – he was the sharp-featured brooder who stared out black-and-whitely from the framed poster on my dining room wall. That Kafka was neurotic Everyman, EveryJew, Every Tortured Writer. Big-eyed, big-eared, serious and thin-faced. He looked like someone destined to die by his own hand, but he did not. He died of tuberculosis and came honestly by his essential frailty – two older brothers, in fact, his only brothers, died as children. Blame, as placed by Kafka (by *the* Kafka, the only Kafka of my concern, so easy to forget that his whole family was Kafka): on Mama Kafka, sweet, almost-gentle Julie, who turned her back on her children in order to work at the Kafka store with Kafka père, placating him, selling ribbons and bows, fabric, buttons, belts.

Kafka, my dining-room-wall brooder, looks like a Wisenberg. Like my father in his old Navy pictures. Except my father was smiling, proud, slightly embarrassed by the starched white uniform. Welcome to the family, Franz. You'll fit right in. He looks like my cousin Jeff, a thin runner with a soft voice who succeeds in business and has a wife, two girl children with bows in their hair. Looks like me, before I was sixteen, before the nose job, the scarification rite of passage for females like me in the 1970s. The question wasn't why, but when. Preferably, during a long vacation.

2. KAFKA, THE JEW AT THE TEA PARTY

Kafka at forty, framed on my wall, is wearing a suit jacket. He is white collar, twentieth century. Like us. The cosmopolitan man. He used the telephone. Took the train, perhaps carried a satchel like the one you have there. Worked at a desk.

Was so modern he might have died in the twentieth-century inventions of the Great Beast, left a camp through a chimney, as his sisters, as his friend Milena Jesenská did. Numbered.

He cared for clothes – he was a flaneur of sorts, a dandy, his father in retail. Dapper. A young man we might take home with us. Meet the folks. A lawyer with a steady income. Who writes in his spare time. A lovely hobby, Mr. Kafka – screen writing or what? Can I get you something for that cough? Hot tea? Caf or herbal? Here's Bengal Spice, or would you prefer Mama Bear's Cold Care, a squeeze of lemon, a spoonful of honey, USDA approved, may contain honey from the U.S., Canada, and Argentina – two continents, imagine that.

And where are your people from, Mr. Kafka? Prague, a lovely city, like Paris of the 1920s, they're saying, just the place for a young writer trying to make his mark. The buildings, they say, so historic, untouched by the war, and the bridges – all that stone, those gargoyles, sunsets, guitar players, how lovely it must be.

Kafka called Prague "the little mother with claws." Like Freud and his Vienna, Kafka hated the town he was most associated with – and stayed there most of his life. He traveled some, went to the country a handful of times and to a sanitarium for his TB. Even went hiking, according to Milena Jesenská. Though he drove her nuts – a man who counted his change. He was on vacation with her when he gave a beggar a two-crown piece and asked for one crown back.

3. KAFKA: THE PUNCH LINE FROM EUROPE

When is a Czech not a Czech?

When is a man at home not at home? When he's born in Prague in the days of the Austro-Hungarian Empire. When he's part of the German-speaking minority of Prague. A majority – about eighty-five percent – Jewish. His work, in fact, was translated from his native German into Czech by the young and beautiful Jesenksá, who also wrote his obituary.

His father, though, burly Herrmann, was another story. Herrmann grew up in a peasant shack, speaking Czech. But he knew German. He used his bilingualism to speak badly of others – he disparaged his Czech-speaking staff in his notions store, discussing them in German with his wife.

4. KAFKA: MULTICULT FIGURE

Summer of 1992, I have come to Europe on fellowship money and am in Prague because it is Prague; I am in the city during this particular week because I have found a conference to attend there. The subject is anti-Semitism in the former Soviet bloc, and the meeting is sponsored by the American Jewish Committee and the Franz Kafka Society. At first I suspect that most of us in the audience are pretending it was the subject, not the city, that drew us. Of course the planners banked on the cachet of Prague. Only years later do I recognize the reputations of the conference speakers. I keep seeing their names in bibliographies and footnotes and on library shelves.

The meeting takes place in a conference center near the end of a streetcar line. Most of the talk is of contemporary pogroms, public opinion surveys in Romania and Germany, the culpability of the Catholic Church. At one point there is a heated tangle over whether a certain 1960s-era Communist was a traitor. We are provided with earphones, simultaneous translations in English, German, Czech, Slovak and Russian; you can figure out the audience members' languages according to when they laugh at the speakers' jokes. I meet Americans at the conference, who, like me, have no standing, so in compensation we take voluminous notes and look very thoughtful.

Postconference, Ellen, one of my new American friends, and I are sitting in the Kafka Society office in Prague. We are taking notes in English on Kafka the native son made good, but it is apparent that he is really Kafka the symbol. The Czechoslovak official from the Czechoslovak Kafka Society tells us that, in effect, our Kafka and the world's Kafka is not their Kafka. Their Kafka is the man from the underground: His work was banned by the Communists, was circulated in samizdat form. Their Kafka is a ghost from early in the century, from the last gasp of multiculturalism in the third city of the fading and former Austro-Hungarian Empire.

Kafka, world-famous after death, was a marginal figure in a marginal society, odd man out. He was part of the spirit excised by Fascists I and II, the humanist buried under the Berlin Wall who crawled through the first fissures. The Czechoslovaks of the Franz Kafka Society want to reclaim that singularness, that one man/one voice. The official is saying, in essence, We are all Kafka.

For them, Kafka was freedom.

Kafka is their America.

What frustrates the Society official is lack of space for the Franz

Kafka Society offices and library. Laws contradict each other, he says, he's been promised the eighteenth-century Kinsky Palace, the building where Kafka went to secondary school, but a museum is settled there, and it would take thousands of dollars to restore the building.

Three stories down from where we are sitting is the town square; arcades where Czechs and Slovaks sell T-shirts and post cards emblazoned with Kafka's likeness, where tourists buy cigarettes and watch the mechanical figures on the town hall clock go through their motions every quarter-hour, and occasionally see a real bride and groom ride up in a genuine horse-drawn carriage and alight the stairs for a civil ceremony. Nearby is the hotel where Kafka's parents were married 110 years ago.

We are not interested, says the official, in Kafka's relationship with his father or the metaphysical meanings of his literary symbols.

They want the man. Their democrat from the grave. Kafka slept here!

(however uneasily)

Is it the writings you love? they ask.

I wish it were the writings. It is the life and not the life. It is the self-doubt. The fears. It is the promise of afterlife. What is it all for? asks the depressive. Kafka answers. You can be sad, says my dining-room picture of Kafka, and still amount to something. You too – with your small recognition and mild successes, whispers this big-eyed, big-eared cousin from the Old Country – can be famous.

5. KAFKA, MAN WITH A JOB

One early evening another new American friend and I find the state insurance office where Kafka worked. We attempt to communicate with the caretaker in pidgin Czech and German. All we seem to understand from the man is something we translate as, "a shame, a shame."

This was where Kafka worked from 1908 to 1922, and during some of that time he was in love with Jesenská. She, according to Jana Çerna's *Kafka's Milena*, "attracted Kafka through those qualities of hers that were the opposite of his: her zest, her thirst for life . . . but in spite of the closeness of their epistolary relationship, Kafka was reluctant to visit her [again] in Vienna. He feared, besides other things, the lying he would have to do at his office in order to be given time off."

Kafka's Milena, at first blush, was a wholesome Czech who filled her apartment with plants so that it resembled a jungle, who wrote about socialism but also about fashion, who once wrote an essay, "The Duty to Feel Joy." Beautiful, girlish, slender Milena Jesenská, with rosy cheeks and curly hair.

A few years after Kafka died, Jesenská became addicted to morphine and would send her young daughter alone to procure drugs from far-flung pharmacies. She became bloated, blowzy, she limped, she regained her girlish figure only after she'd been imprisoned during the Nazi takeover of Czechoslovakia. She became a victim of the Great Beast: Ravensbrück, 1944.

6. KAFKA: THE GHOST IN A CEMETERY

In the Jewish quarter, the cemetery is familiar – perhaps, from pictures – tombstones leaning and crowded like broken gray teeth, and packed with tourists. Some loud Germans are sitting on a bench just inside the entrance and smoking cigarettes. I chastise them in French. French is where I hide. I feel that if I spoke English, they would know I was Jewish, would be able to tell, despite my 1972 nose job, that I am just another American Jew who came to Europe to wag her finger in the faces of Nazis or approximations thereof. While the French – well, French Jews were put to death during the war, and only in this decade, it seems, are the French owning up to their part in it. I'd rather be thought a French citizen of the world insisting on due respect in a *cimetière*, maintaining the proprieties. *Tout comme il faut* and all that.

The Germans put out their cigarettes.

The old cemetery is not Kafka's final resting place. For that you have to take a subway about eight stops out from the center of town to a large parklike cemetery, unkempt in back like so many other Jewish cemeteries on the continent (You know why, don't you? No one left to tend them.) At the front, where the older graves are, there's a sign, "Dr. Franz Kafka – 21.14.33" and an arrow pointing to the right. Did he die so late, 1933? Or was it 1921? Then I realize that there's no fourteenth month, these numbers are guides to his plot. Then there's a sign attached to a tree: "Kafka, 400 m." His plain tombstone has a skinny pine tree in front of it, standing amid gravel, his name above those of his parents.

He died at forty, the age he was in my poster at home. I take out a polished blue pebble, bought on the street in Berkeley, for Kafka. That's the way Jews show respect for the dead, our people's way of saying, I was here, an ancient way of marking a grave.

Go away, says his grave. You can try to prettify the granite with a small blue stone but death is death. Finis.

What did I expect? At the base of the tombstone are a handful of bouquets and a pot of pale purple petunias. I copy as carefully as I can the unfamiliar words at the base: *Na pamět. . . . za nacistické okupace v Létech 1942–43. Gabriela Herrmanová nar. 22.9.1899; Valerie Polláková, nar. 25.9.1890; Otilie Davidová, nar. 29.10.1892.* In other words, I take it, his sisters died sometime in 1942 or '43.

Some other tourists are coming, young scruffy boys. I walk away. I have nothing else to say to the dead Kafkas.

Where is the Kafka poster from? they ask. Why do you have it on your dining room wall?

I bought it in New York at the Jewish Museum. I think that was the trip where I stopped in the New Yorker *office and talked to editors because they'd just accepted a story of mine. I was newly thirty-three. A month before when the postman had come to my door with a big gray envelope from the* New Yorker, *I had said, This will change my life.*

Now I'm forty.

Or maybe it was the trip before or before.

7. KAFKA, REMAINS

Franz Kafka: lover manqué of Milena Jesenksá. Son manqué of a businessman; the family sold notions; the trademark of the family store was a jackdaw, which in Czech is *kavka.*

jackdaw: a kind of crow – *Corvus monedula,* "which frequents church towers, old buildings, etc.; noted for its loquacity and thievish propensities." (*The Shorter Oxford English Dictionary,* 1933)

When Prague hoodlums went on an anti-Jewish rampage during Kafka's boyhood, they spared Herrmann Kafka's store because they assumed robust papa was Czech, one of them. He was like them, a man of the people, a man who knew merchandise, rubbed fabric between his fingers, dealt in – I imagine, I conjure – grosgrain, satin, cottons, taffetas, silks, pins, buttons, threads, clasps, needles, thimbles, hooks and eyes, threads dyed in all colors, coarse and fine, light and dark, what will it be today, madam, and a bow for the young missus?

What happened to the owners of the clothes made from the bolts of cloth whose ravaging was staved off by the strength of Herrmann Kafka's rough charm? What happened to the hooks and eyes, the cloth-covered buttons, the velvets and eyelets and frogs?

What happened to the carefully sewn borders of your grandmother's Alençon lace wedding gown?

What happened to your father's *tallis*, your great-aunt's velvet cloak, your mother's high-heeled dyed-to-match pumps of raw silk?

Where is your baby dress and christening robe?

In Prague in the grand square, I visit a little Kafka museum. Under glass there are Jewish artifacts – the type of which were used in a Jewish home such as Kafka's, say the tags.

In a Czech village called Wossek, Kafka's papa grew up in poverty with six brothers and sisters. According to Kafka biographer Ernst Pawel, the family's one-room shack was still inhabited after World War II, outlasting many Czechs, Jews, Kafkas.

Today Czechoslovakia is divided and ripe for development, the playwright Havel has a ceremonial post. His jazz albums and chandeliers wink at us in color from *Architectural Digest*. Take me, the country says to investors; "Take me," Czecho/slovakia says, in German and in English, "and bring me a tall decaf Frappuccino while you're at it."

§

The uniqueness of the jackdaw is that it can be taught to speak.

Who wouldn't want one, for your very own, it would sit on your shoulder, pluck grains from your palm, repeat to you your secrets, whisper in your ear all that you know.

Holocaust Girls/Closet

Nazis came to Texas in the 1960s. We could hear them just around the corner. My older sister Rosi would make the sound of their foot-steps – would tap her hands on the pink carpet of the walk-in closet in her room (just like the one in mine). She would look up and say, "Listen, do you hear them?" I would hold my breath. We were in the woods with the partisans. Though we didn't know the exact meaning of the word. We sat around our (invisible) campfire. We were hiding from the Nazis. They would take us away. We had saltines and olives to live on.

Sometimes I would be the one to tap tap tap slap my palms against the pink carpet: "Listen, do you hear them?" Nazis coming through the woods. They had been tipped off, perhaps by paid informers, like the ones who had turned in Anne Frank.

I had read her diary. We had seen the end of the movie on TV though my mother had said, "Don't you think they should go to bed?" My father had said, "They have to learn." What we had to learn about was life. What had happened to the Jews crouched in silence.

On TV we heard the big Nazi boot against the door of the Secret Annex where the Franks had hidden. The Nazis bashed in the door the way ours had never been bashed, or my father's or my mother's. My father had fought the Nazis in the ocean. My mother had stayed home. She'd been a schoolgirl.

Once I asked her, "Have you ever had a raw potato?" I imagined her digging them from a field, getting through the war. She'd grown up in Dallas. She said, "Maybe once" – when her brother's barbe-cue project in the back yard hadn't turned out. Potato half-raw, half-burned. There was no starvation, no SS in Texas. No hiding with par-tisans. Nothing but two daughters in the 1960s with saltines and green olives stuffed with pimientos, and sometimes a strand or two of raw spaghetti to munch on.

For years I kept a getaway bag in my closet – saltines and a notebook, a change of clothes. An alarm clock, so I would know the time. I liked the big, friendly white and gold face of that alarm clock. One summer night the air conditioning didn't work and we opened the windows and I heard Nazis, scratching to get in to take me away and steal my glasses. In the morning my father claimed the noise had been mosquitoes, other night insects. June bugs. The same June bugs I would watch at night on the porch. I would turn over the June bugs that had landed on their backs, skittering. I wanted to right all the June bugs.

We liked playing in the closet. We liked the thrill of hiding. We were victims but we were never caught. Sometimes we played secretary instead. Sometimes we played that we were lizards on a ship hiding from the Nazis. The Nazis would take us to a concentration camp. They would take my glasses and asthma drugs and let death just come up and kill me, like that. At Hebrew school the teachers talked about Nazis. They showed us a film on a small screen. They showed us the small bodies and the striped prison outfits. But we didn't think of it as prison. It was a death camp and the Nazis took people there. Jews.

They didn't take us because we were quiet in the woods, we sprinkled sand and dirt over our fire in the closet in the woods before they were close enough to smell the smoke. The Nazis were stupid. They were thick and dumb like animals and wore big heavy boots up to their hips. We were good so the Nazis would never find us. We were smarter and darker than the Nazis. But we were bad, something bad about us or the Nazis wouldn't be after us in the first place.

When we played secretary, our office was out in the hall and we would hold papers up to the air vents that would suck them so they stuck. When we played school, the air vents held up the pretend tests we gave each other. Sometimes we would just play without having a name to it and slide across the terrazzo floor in our stocking feet. We didn't wear shoes when we hid from the Nazis. They would find us; shoes would make too much noise.

Sometimes at dusk we played capture-the-flag with the neighbor kids in the Shelbys' front yard. After a rain we'd play stand-in-old-shoes-in-the-mud-in-the-side-yard. Sometimes we'd go to the houses still being built and stand on the extra lumber and play island-in-the-ocean. There were brown rabbits in the "empty" lot behind the house and once policemen came with horses back there on a search for someone – a criminal hiding in the overgrown weeds.

At some point we stopped playing Nazi. It wasn't my idea to start or stop. Maybe Rosi stopped playing with me, started playing with her own friends, and no more Nazis. We outgrew Nazis. When I was twenty-one I went to Amsterdam and went, alone, to the Secret Annex. It was on the tourist map. Each room was small and there was a guest book to sign with a fancy gold pen, unattached to anything, no string or chain. There were the books Anne Frank had read while she was in hiding and her movie star pictures pinned to the wall. The place was small, it had no power, too many people walking through.

Ten years after that, on a layover in the Amsterdam airport, a Greek man saw me borrow someone's tour book of the Anne Frank house. The Greek man said to his American wife: "Of course she's interested in Anne Frank – she's Jewish." The man who'd bought the book wasn't Jewish. I said nothing. The Greek had been able to tell that I was Jewish.

There is a statue of Anne Frank in front of a church in Amsterdam. In the walk-in closets in Houston now are full-length mirrors and the shelves that Rosi and I covered in our favorite pink contact paper, ruffles that we tacked along the edges. The closets are shrines, and storage. In Rosi's closet are my mother's mink coat and the large bride doll too big to play with and the felt board with felt numbers.

Where I live now I don't sit in closets. The closets are full. I'm on the third floor. No Nazis bang against my screens at night. Around the world people are defacing Jewish graves, threatening pogroms. In my neighborhood Jewish Community Center I watched a slide show of someone's trip to Europe – pictures of Auschwitz-Birkenau, rust-colored gas chamber. "It was cold," the traveler told us, "so very very cold. Everyone told us to bring our sweaters, even though it was a warm day." Ghosts breathing out cold air, having absorbed the force of someone's bare hatred. About 175 miles from the camp, the traveler had seen two young boys spray-paint on a memorial to the Warsaw Ghetto. She said, "There is hatred for Jews where there are not even Jews any more."

Anne Frank was shipped from Auschwitz-Birkenau to Bergen-Belsen. I read about her all through my childhood. She never seemed like a child to me. At parties I eat olives and crackers. Alone at night, shadows brush against my face. At the JCC, one of the slides showed words in a foreign language carved into a wall at the concentration camp. The traveler thought it said to never forget. In my late twenties when I felt sad I would go to the public library and read *Anne Frank: The Diary of a Young Girl*. It was warm and familiar. It would soothe me.

FLYING

Dinnertime at the artists' colony and we sit in the historic house around a possibly historic table, talking about dreams, flying in them. I never fly in mine, I say, but then I remember: floating a few feet above the sidewalk. Walking on air. Bounding. And more: in dreams I appreciate flying while I'm in the midst of it, I remind myself not to forget to notice it.

Such floating is a gift.

Sometimes I bob like Ed Wynn in *Mary Poppins* – my head grazes the top of a covered bridge, dodging wet paint, rusty edges. The fantastic is not always without consequences.

The food at that dinner – who remembers? Or precisely who was there? In a house none of us grew up in. Candles, conversations that slowed then sped up. Three blond wooden tables pushed together, in a rich tidy town north of Chicago in the 1990s. Near the lake. Was it winter? Summer? Behind the house, unseen, in the prairie somewhere, surely there were deer.

§

In Prague, 1992, I found my way to performance art – first a long tram ride, then a walk down curving streets until I came upon a line of smokers in black, wearing skinny eyeglasses – hip in any language. I talked my way into the sold-out theater, then saw that everyone else was finally let in too. I cannot describe the performance, though I took notes. It was in Russian, the second language every Czechoslovak took in school. Smoke on stage, and dancing, actors in red, a song by Edith Piaf.

How can I explain that it was captivating? And evanescent? Afterwards, I went on a crazed car ride with a lesbian–Czech–Reform Jew (Yes, we had a Reform synagogue here before the United States did, she said proudly, severely; in fact, Kafka's father was on the synagogue board) and her gay friend. The actors must have flown on stage or spoken of flying – I've forgotten now – because the man in the car said, I would like to fly, and the woman said, You do fly, when you have sex.

We went from place to place, a kaleidoscopic evening, careening from one building to the next: a house where I spoke French to someone who gave us apples, the messy office of an avant-garde magazine, a gay bar where I picked up AIDS pamphlets in Czech to send to a friend in El Salvador. All night I – native English speaker, granddaughter of East European Jewish immigrants, hetero so far – was with foreigners. Everything resembled something else. I did not know what anyone's life was like there, but I could guess. (I dream in French. I dream of women.) At the gay bar, I talked so easily to the American men. My *landslayt*.

At the performance the Czechoslovaks had heard the language of the Great Bear used by those who flew across the stage, or wanted to. *Je ne regrette rien*, sang Edith Piaf, sounding as if on a gramophone, a decades-old recording. I sat in the audience among the young people of Prague I would never see again, hearing what they were hearing, watching the same stage – so separated from them, but there, among them, my body, theirs.

§

In Chicago, N. (Skokie-born, son of survivors) sits in my dining room after the other guests have left. We are listening to Enya and he tells me about his dating life. There was the woman, he says, he had sex with but she seemed to disappear. I wonder if another man sits in another dining room telling a friend about a woman – me – who once disappeared in his arms, his bed. Another friend, a lover manqué, once told me of a woman he could not kiss right, their styles too foreign, their tongues never in synch, but later in the conversation he said, We sleep together. And she comes, he added, but it seems like she's not there. Another woman gone missing.

Where does she go? Where is he not able to follow her? What hole does she slip down? Where does her soul leap to? Does she hover above the bed, walking lightly above her diminished self?

Where does sex go when it's finished? What happens to the air that no longer supports your weight? Where does desire return from? The first and last night of great sex with H. I was afraid, of going down into the kiva, some cave, a country that would not stamp my passport. I thought, How can you return to ordinary life after this? And how can it stop? And how can it not stop? How could you do this more than once in any lifetime?

§

Once at a drum circle in Berkeley I disappeared into the sound and was afraid to stay for another drumming session. Afraid it wouldn't be the same, that I would be bored. I was too attached to the experience, the Zen masters would say.

More, I want more. And am afraid.

§

In graveyards all across Central Europe I searched for headstones that said Wisenberg or Rachofsky or Mindel, for relatives to reclaim, but all along mourned my father, dead for a year. He was with me, I could feel him, over my shoulders, just watching, waiting for me to recognize him in each new place. I am sorry you died, I said to him. I am sorry I didn't know you, couldn't find the key to knowing you, went at it clumsily, asking questions directly, tried to force open the door at its hinges. Told you nothing of myself, did not tell you that I am afraid of flying away, or that when I see lighted buildings at night, when the sky turns cobalt, I feel my soul take a breath, I come close to crying.

§

With A., I soar. I want to love him. I sigh and sigh, and when it's his turn for focused pleasure he must direct me: slow, fast, there, there. We are not flying. We are grounded. Like high school, he grumbles. Though that time was not without its charms.

§

Night after night I could not touch H. I saw ghosts, devils. I craved a touch, but did not know whose.

§

In Prague I thought, Do I fly during sex? Does she fly higher than I do? Does he?

§

I'm walking on air, lovers sing, I'm ten feet high. I'm on top of the world.

With D., we would hold hands and skip across cracks in the pavement. We'd shout, Leap! until it was no longer a verb, or a command, just sound.

§

I wish I could tell you exactly how it was, in that shabby-chic neighborhood theater in Prague, in the nation that had not yet split in two,
how I couldn't understand the language on stage but was absorbed by
the sound, the movement, but I can't tell you, it's like giving a report
of someone else's dream. It's the way no architect could ever repro-
duce the theater building itself – recreate the layers of it, complete
with traces of what it had been used for before, and before that, and
before that – no matter how many times she or he were to subject the
paint scrapings and wood samples to examination.

§

I wish I could tell you what went wrong, each time something went
wrong, and what I did right – what worked, why and how, and make
blueprints to remember and keep. If I could hold knowledge in me,
let it guide me. If I could go back, to each nuance, each movement,
back to the cold unmade bed, middle of the night, do it right, fly, back
to the scene of the crime, get it there, leap over awkwardness, take a
deep breath and fly, into his arms, out of this world, into a foreign
language, a place you can't describe, elusive, evanescent, unforgetta-
ble, untranslatable, singing then and forever that I regret nothing,
carry nothing with me, elated, light, bobbing under bridges while
the sky is the best blue – cobalt, and I float over pavement, along the
smoky outer walls of smooth-planed buildings, fires roaring inside,
rooms golden inside, and me unafraid of floating upwards forever
into the endless sky

The Language of *Heimatlos*

The Dandy

The young man from Germany arrives in Paris illegally, by train. It is 1936. He brings with him little money and little French. Relatives take him in, provide him with pocket money. He goes on trips to the countryside, organized by the Jewish community, where he brags to a young woman that he walked the whole way from Hanover, Germany, to Paris. Back in the City of Lights, he and his best friend see the latest films. *Morocco, Michael Strogoff*. He has no *petite amie*. He is not adept with the French language. He does not have a job, lives off his hardworking aunt and uncle, who have a tailor shop. He smokes three packs of cigarettes a week. He gets his news from the Yiddish daily paper his uncle brings home. The news is not good. He and his friend Nathan escape to the movies: *Ben Hur. Dark Eyes*. He likes love stories. Westerns, adventure.

He wants to be a flaneur, a dandy. Man of the world. Carefree, a boulevardier, a man who owns the streets. He can't always afford to sit inside his favorite café, which is called Tout Va Bien – all goes well, all is well. He and his friends meet on the sidewalk in front.

Perhaps he dreams of consorting with Marlene Dietrich and Simone Simon, whose faces and gestures he's learned well from the movies. Alas, he is not as suave as Gary Cooper. His French is still broken, his English nonexistent. His dance partners are émigré girls. He is a Polish Jew lacking finesse, and papers.

He was born in Hanover, Germany, but he is not a German Jew. He is an *Ausländer*, foreigner, because his parents are from the East. They fled further and further west, from pogroms and threat of pogroms, from a land of unrest to Prussia, where they were issued coveted residence permits. He and his family are *Ostjuden* – Eastern Jews. This word is rarely said kindly. The *Ostjude* speaks Yiddish, a *zhargon*, a language of the kitchen and shop, a language mocked and disdained by the outside world, including many native-born German Jews. This is the language of the young man, the language of the immigrants of Hanover and Paris, his first language, his *mameloshn*, mother tongue. At the end of the century, Yiddish will be lovingly restored and embraced by the remnants, but that is much later, when there are few Ostjuden to populate the ghettos of Europe.

TWO KINDS OF JEWS

The stereotype of the Ostjude: male. He wore black and ate garlic, had large families, lived in tenements, spoke Yiddish, did not mix in well. Made all Jews look bad by association. Before the war, this is what the cultured Jews, the German-speaking Jews, the Goethe-quoting, urban-apartment-living, brief-case-toting, university-educated, dash-into-a-synagogue-now-and-then Jews would say: The Ostjude "was totally alien to me, alien in every utterance, in every breath, and when he failed to rouse my sympathy for him as a human being he even repelled me. . . ." So wrote the novelist Jacob Wassermann in his 1921 memoir, *My Life as German and Jew.*

(Years later German Jews who loved their Homeland gave their lives for it – because they could not believe that anyone, even Hitler, could imagine a *Heimat* – homeland – without them in it.)

Hitler wrote in *Mein Kampf*, "Once, as I was strolling through the Inner City [in Vienna], I suddenly encountered an apparition in a black caftan and black hair locks. Is this a Jew? was my first thought. . . . Is this a German?"

Theodor Herzl, the well-polished founder of Zionism, assumed that although there would be opera in many languages in the new land of Palestine, German would serve as the day-to-day lingua franca. He imagined that in the promised land, the Eastern, Yiddish-speaking Jews would become robust by working in the fields, would become jolly and brown, and, of course, German-speaking.

I am an Ostjude. But by the time I was born in Texas, about ten years after the end of the war everyone wanted to forget, it didn't matter. I was middle class, the child of the children of immigrants. The child of the children of children of U.S. citizens. English was my first language; how could it have been any different? My mother and father remembered the snobbery of the German Jews, but it was slight. The normative Jews were the ones like us. Growing up I felt alienated – by personality and temperament, not by background – among the other

Baby Boomers whose grandparents had emigrated from Eastern Europe, like mine had.

I didn't know that Yiddish was once considered as the possible official language of Palestine, before Hebrew, enlivened and modernized, won out. (Herzl was long dead by then.) At Hebrew school in Houston the pedagogy-deprived Israeli teachers taught us to dismiss our parents' Ashkenazi (European) pronunciation of Hebrew, in favor of the Sephardic that was favored in Israel. I learned to say "*tof*" where my father read "*sof.*" Our parents said "Shabes," we said "Shabbat." After services on the holidays all generations said to their family and friends, automatically, "Good *yontev.*" Happy holiday. Much later I realized that the phrase was Yiddish and that it was "*gut,*" not "good."

In Israel, the founding Jews were mostly Ashkanazi – Ostjuden as well as the urban, professional German-speakers. Both the German and Eastern European Jews have become the elite there. The poorer Jews have been another kind of Eastern Jew, Sephardic, from North Africa and other Muslim countries, with darker skin, less education, more children, but whose pronunciation of Hebrew was considered more authentic. Now the Sephardim's star is rising.

THE WAR FROM THIS SIDE

During the Holocaust my most immediate relatives were in Houston, Dallas, Austin, Omaha, Baltimore, and in the service. My father was in the Navy, my mother was in high school and college. Relatives, those whose names we no longer knew, died. Must have died. The ones left behind in Kishinev, in Slutsk, in a little shtetl near Kovno called Pusvatin: great-grandparents and great-great uncles, cousins three and four times removed. If not them, then their friends, neighbors, close as family itself.

When I was growing up, there was only one kosher bakery in town. It was run by short, sharp foreign bakers who were brothers. I knew the son of one of them from school. The bakers were not friendly. They scared me with their unfamiliarity. They were survivors. Looking back, I wonder if there were class differences, too, but I have no idea what their background was, what their lives were like back in, presumably, Poland. We saw films about the Holocaust in

Hebrew school, we spoke of it with a hush in our voices. One third of us, our people, died. There was the mystery of Death. There was the allure of the drama as well. The idea that we could have been part of a catastrophe that was historic. And we were. Just as we said every Friday in the Kiddush over the wine, when we blessed God for bringing us out of Egypt, where we were slaves.

DARK EYES

I have thick dark curly hair and brown eyes. No one believes me when I say I'm from Texas. They say, Oh, aren't you from New York? When I travel in Europe, people don't believe that I'm American. They question me further: "Where were your parents born?" When I tell them Texas, Mississippi, they go back another generation, asking about my grandparents. And are satisfied only when I say that my grandparents and great-grandparents are from Eastern Europe. Lithuania. Moldova. The look on their faces says, Why didn't you save time and say that in the first place?

Who are these people who ask? A man on a bus in Istanbul. A security guy in Paris. This is that story: It was summer 1997. I was standing in front of an eighteenth-century building, the residence of the German ambassador to France. I held a notebook, carried a red backpack, wore walking shoes – looked harmless, as usual. The head of security passed by, figured I was Italian or Spanish. And harmless. I asked him about the building, said I was writing about the assassination that took place there in 1938. He invited me in. Polished floors, oil paintings, chandeliers. I took pictures.

The young man in Paris, the not-German dandy from Germany, was the assassin. His name was Herschel Grynszpan. In the fall of 1938 he was seventeen, five feet tall, about one hundred pounds, with rosebud lips and dark hair. In 1938, he was still in Paris, hiding from the French authorities because his residence permit had expired. On November 3, he received a postcard from his sister Berta. She, her brother Mordechai, and their parents had been deported from Hanover in the first mass transport of Jews out of Germany. Though their parents, Sendel and Rivka Grynszpan, had lived in Germany since 1911, they were not citizens. They were born Russian subjects but had opted for Polish citizenship when Poland became independent.

Thousands of Polish-born Jews lived in the Reich – which included Austria after the annexation of March 1938. The Polish government had become afraid that as Hitler tightened the noose around Jews in the Reich, the Jews who were technically Polish would return to Poland. To prevent that, Poland revoked the citizenship of any Pole who had not lived in the country for the past five years.

The Grynszpans were wanted by neither Germany nor Poland – officially, *heimatlos*. Stateless. Without *Heimat*, homeland, fatherland. "Displaced person" and "illegal immigrant" lack the punch of "heimatlos." Without a place to belong. Defined by what you don't have.

Because they were officially not Poles, they were not Germans, they were Jews who belonged nowhere, Herschel's parents, brother and sister, and twelve thousand other Jews from throughout Germany were taken from their homes and left in a chill, empty cleared-away area in a Polish-German no-man's-land. Their passports were out of date, they couldn't apply for new ones because no government wanted to claim them. These twelve thousand Jews were Polish-, Russian-, Galician-, and Ukrainian-born Yiddish-speakers (parents) and German-born German speakers (children) with no place to lay their heads down at night. The lucky ones were sheltered in stables and pigsties. The Grynszpans found shelter in a military stable full of horse manure. Winter was coming soon. Local Jews in the border town of Zbaszyn took in some of the refugees.

A few days later Berta mailed another postcard to Herschel in Paris: Send money.

Back when he lived in Germany, Herschel's classmates had called him Maccabee, after the ancient Jewish warrior family, because he was hot-tempered and ready to fight. In Paris, on November 6, 1938, according to some versions of the story, the seventeen year old argues with his guardian, his Uncle Abraham, about money. It seems that Herschel's father sent Uncle Abraham three thousand francs for Herschel's upkeep. Herschel wants to send the money right away to his family in Zbaszyn. Abraham wants to assess the situation first. He wants to wait, Herschel is too young to wait, the situation too dire for waiting, these are his parents and brother and sister, he would be there with them in no-man's-land if he hadn't left them; if only he'd been able to find a job in Hanover like his hard-working family members, he'd be there with them, now, in a cold barn. The uncle and nephew in Paris argue and Herschel leaves the apartment in anger, not forgetting two hundred francs' allowance that his uncle has given him. That night he checks into a hotel down the street from El Dorado, a dance club he's frequented. His uncle looks for him to no avail. In the morning Herschel walks down the street to a small gun shop just opening for the day, buys a revolver and bullets. He loads it in the bathroom of Café Tout Va Bien. Descends into the Métro, exits at Solférino, near the symbol and locus of all the evil that has befallen his family – the German embassy – and tells the receptionist he has private business to discuss. A document.

He is shown to the office of the third secretary, Ernst vom Rath, twenty-nine years old. There Herschel shouts at him: "You are a filthy kraut, and here, in the name of twelve thousand persecuted Jews, is your document!" And he shoots at the man five times.

The long-haired German security man gave me a copy in French of a book about the history of the building. The events of November 1938 are told in the words of the ambassador from 1936 to 1939, who refers to tension in political life during his tenure. Of the events of November 1938, he says only, "Before the hours of reception, a young man asked to talk to the ambassador, and because I was crossing the courtyard of the embassy, he was, according to custom, introduced instead to the highest official present; then he killed him with many revolver bullets. The embassy lost a serious and distinguished employee." [my translation]
That's it.

French police arrested Herschel without a struggle.
Dorothy Thompson, the newspaper columnist and radio commentator, made him a cause célèbre. From America she started a journalists' defense fund for him, cautiously making sure that all contributors were Gentile.

Vom Rath lingered in a Paris hospital for two days, during which time he received a blood transfusion from a French World War I hero, and was promoted from third secretary to counsel of the legation.

(He was a lawyer.) He died on November 9. At the memorial service in Paris, an official called vom Rath the Reich's first martyr. He said, "Commence the journey to the homeland."

November 9 was also the fifteenth anniversary of Hitler's beer hall putsch. It was Goebbels' idea to order "spontaneous" pogroms throughout the Reich to celebrate the anniversary and take vengeance on the Jews. November 9–10, 1938, became known as Reichskristallnacht, or Kristallnacht, the night of broken glass, the night when Jewish property was attacked throughout Germany and what had been Austria.

At least ten thousand Jews, including longstanding citizens of Germany and Austria, were sent to Buchenwald and tortured. The estimated toll: 90 Jews killed, 7,500 Jewish businesses gutted, 190 synagogues destroyed, 30,000 wealthy Jews sent to concentration camps. An insurance company told the Nazi regime that the amount of glass broken equaled two years of Belgian production – that country was the only supplier of plate glass for windows in Germany. Jewish property owners were entitled to insurance money for damages. The Nazis didn't want Jews compensated in any way for Kristallnacht so they required Jewish inhabitants to pay a fine of one billion marks to the Reich. And they confiscated the insurance claims.

Thus the German Jews were shown incontrovertibly that though they considered themselves good Germans, their passports did bear the letter J, their middle names were officially Israel or Sarah, and they could suffer the same fate as the Ostjuden.

Just as Polish Jews were beginning to feel at home in Germany, they were shown that they were neither Germans nor Poles, but something in between.

It was Herschel's fault but not his fault. The Nazi regime was looking for an excuse. If not for Herschel, Hitler and his henchmen would have found another scapegoat. There is evidence: in 1938 more uniforms were ordered to be on hand at concentration camps, as well as more yellow cloth from which to make patches for the Jews. It is probable, writes retired U.S. State Department staffer Gerald Schwab in *The Day the Holocaust Began: The Odyssey of Herschel Grynszpan*, that if not for Kristallnacht, there would have been some other "dramatic repression" by summer 1939.

"Herschel Grynszpan, in retrospect," muses Schwab in 1999,

"saved a lot more lives than he harmed." Schwab is talking to me on the phone from his home in Alexandria, Virginia. He says that Herschel's act sped the emigration of German Jews . . . like the Schwabs. "I doubt if I would be alive if it weren't for Kristallnacht."

TERRORISTS

A dozen years before Herschel's bullets killed vom Rath, a Ukrainian-born Jew, Samuel Schwartzbard, killed Simon Petliura, an exiled Ukrainian leader, in cold blood outside of Chartier restaurant in Paris. Under Petliura's short leadership of Ukraine, from 1919 to 1921, at least fifty thousand Jews had been killed. Schwartzbard was more settled in France than Herschel was. He had become a citizen, had received the Croix de Guerre, which he wore in court. In his trial Schwartzbard admitted the act was predetermined. In his summation, his attorney proclaimed, "No, it is no longer you, Schwartzbard, who is the cause here; it is the pogroms."

Schwartzbard was found not guilty. He died in 1938 (months before Kristallnacht) while visiting Cape Town, South Africa, and was given a hero's funeral by the Jewish community there.

In 1936 a Jewish medical student from Croatia, David Frankfurter, killed the leader of the Swiss Nazis. Many Jews, including his own father, who was a rabbi, condemned his act. He was imprisoned and then freed in 1945, after serving half of his eighteen-year sentence. He immigrated to Palestine, where he worked for the Ministry of Defense, had a family, and died in 1982.

Starting a few days after vom Rath's assassination, Goebbels and other Nazi leaders linked Grynszpan's crime with Frankfurter's – claiming a Communist-Jewish conspiracy, lamenting another political murder of a loyal German working abroad.

The summer of 1997 in Paris there were trash cans on the street bolted shut. Because of the possibility of bombs. Down in the subway, there were warnings about suspicious packages. Fifty-nine years before, Herschel with his new pistol had entered the Paris subway, exited at Solférino, entered the embassy, and shot five times. Two bullets met his target. Killed an innocent man. As innocent as a card-carrying Nazi party member could be. Vom Rath had joined the party in the early years but was not known to be an anti-Semite.

A Brief History of Heimat

Heimat, by its nature it is indefinable, ungraspable. It is Homeland, the good old days, the way-back-when utopian countryside of the German provinces – the concept originally a reaction to industrialization. It was later taken up by the Nazis – Heimat with a monstrous face. After the Second World War, *Heimatlos* was a hit song, taken to heart by the ethnic Germans who had become refugees. In the 1970s Heimat became a longing for the unpolluted, peaceful simple life, the dream of the Green Party. In 1984 it was a sixteen-hour serial film by Edgar Reitz, seen on TV by at least nine million West Germans. It is the story of four generations in a small town. The focus is on family and friends. You can barely catch glimpses of the Reich in the margins. There is no Auschwitz.

Reitz made the film to counter an American TV series shown in Germany in 1979 – *Holocaust*.

This history is from the 1989 book by German-born Anton Kaes, *From Hitler to Heimat: The Return of History as Film*. I took a seminar from him in Berkeley in 1991. He is married to a German-born woman, they have raised their two children to be good secular citizens of the Bay Area. One day Anton – Tony – told this story: His son came home from school and asked, Are we Jewish? (They aren't.) The point was that the child was so unaware of religion that he assumed he was what his friends were. I doubt that a young Tony or his father would have ever asked such a question.

The Eternal Ostjude

What's the difference between an Eastern Jew and a German Jew?

One generation.

When do you call someone a Polish Jew even if he has never been to Poland?

When he is in the West.

Herschel's father Sendel, or Zyndel or Shmuel, Grynzspan was an Ostjude, born in Dmenin, Poland, in 1886. He married in 1910, and the next year he and his wife, Rivka, headed west, as other Ostjuden had done, believing that they could find relative freedom from persecution and a chance to start over. The newlyweds settled in Hanover, Germany. Sendel worked as a plumber, junk man, and tailor. Herschel was born on March 28, 1921, one of ultimately six or perhaps eight children. Only three of them survived childhood. Herschel was not a good student. He dropped out of school at fourteen, with a certificate that showed only that he attended. He claimed his teachers were anti-Semitic; they said he was lazy. Two books published in 1989 and 1990 provide two different views of the youth. In one, he is lazy, conniving, a show-off. In the other, he is a lost child, very loving and very set upon by circumstances. In both, he is devoted to his family. Before he decided to go to France, Herschel studied in a yeshivah in Frankfurt, not so much for religious reasons as political – he wanted to learn Hebrew, to prepare to emigrate to Palestine. But he changed his mind when an old man told him that Germany was no place for a lad such as himself, and rather than wait around in Germany, Herschel went west in 1936. He stayed with relatives in Belgium first, and they helped him slip into France.

During the preparation of Herschel's trial in France, Hitler appointed a Berlin law professor, Friedrich Grimm, as a "technical adviser" in the Grynszpan case. In Grimm's writings, you can see how Herschel became the epitome of the Ostjude, in line with Nazi prejudices. Herschel, Grimm alleged, considered himself too good for manual labor, "the habitual mentality of all the lower elements, particularly the anarchist Jews of Eastern Europe." He was a product of a troubled milieu of eastern Jews from Poland or Ukraine, who made as much trouble as the Russian Jews, who spread the "Bolshevik virus" into eastern and central Europe. Grimm claimed the Jewish social clubs Herschel frequented were places where Jews were interested in forming fighting groups or gangs.

It was the Grynszpans' fault, also, he said, that they traipsed across Europe, "eternally unsatisfied." The family was primitive, he claimed; neither Herschel's grandmother, mother, nor aunt could read or write, and his Parisian uncle hardly knew how to sign his name in French, Grimm said.

The family was always fighting, generally over money, typical of all

Jews, according to Grimm. Subscribing to Nazi anti-Semitic conspiracy theory, Grimm wrote that Judaism or international Masons directed French politics. And the Communist Party was behind Grynszpan's actions – it was part of organized terrorist Jewry, receiving orders from New York and Moscow, he said. The alleged terrorists included "the half-Jew mayor of New York," Fiorello LaGuardia.

SECURITY

In Paris, the security man and I spoke in English, his second language. He had long hair and wore a black T-shirt and black jeans. When he wasn't working at the ambassador's residence he was a director of a small theater group. He said he'd first gotten into security work as an alternative to military service. He was born near Heidelberg, said the grandfather of his grandfather had been Jewish and converted. One day during the Hitler regime his grandmother went into town to go shopping. Perhaps it was the day of the national boycott of Jewish businesses, April 1, 1933. This is what the long-haired man said: "An asshole said, 'You can't buy there, it's a Jewish store.' She said, 'I'll buy where I want.' The asshole couldn't do anything because my grandfather was a big man in town." The grandfather wouldn't join the Nazi Party so he was sent to fight in Normandy – and survived, becoming mayor after the war.

His parents were members of Pathfinders, a scout-like group (which began expelling Jews from membership in 1933).

It must be hard to be German, I said.

He said, It's not hard if you're stupid.

He asked if I was afraid of Germans.

I said no.

I think I was lying.

I don't think he asked whether I was Jewish. I assumed he could tell that I was. I didn't ask him if he was afraid of Jews.

We were the same. Youngish. Anti-establishment, in the arts, antifascist, modern. Wearers of T-shirts and no discernible religious outerwear. Aging members of the international youth culture.

STREETS OF PARIS

In Paris men on the street would click with the insides of their mouths, they would say, "Bonjour, Mademoiselle." When I didn't answer, they would try, "Buenos días" and "Italiana?" I would shake my head. I hadn't been to Paris in twenty years, since I was twenty-one. Then, when men made remarks on the street, I would be half-pleased. I had not been trained to respond to this sort of thing.

In Paris in the 1970s once or twice in the Métro a man flashed me. It would take me a moment to register what was happening. My disbelief was stronger than my shame, though that was there too. And excitement – they are doing something they are not supposed to do.

There was something wrong with these men. What was it? But at the same time they seemed natural, part of the cityscape. It was difficult to imagine them in their kitchens at home reading the newspaper. They were men without homes, *sans abri*, as if exposing themselves was a way of saying: Look at me, look how unprotected I am.

In the summer of 1997 I didn't see any flashers. By then, at forty-one, I had learned that men who exposed themselves in public weren't harmless but were on the continuum of sexual aggression. At forty-one I had also become less friendly, more guarded. I stopped looking into the eyes of strangers on the street. Once, though, I forgot, and when I stepped out of one of those bulky new public toilets on the street, a man caught my eye and asked, "Ça va?" Are things all right?

HERSCHEL AS HISTORY

He is barely mentioned in general accounts of the Holocaust. In one of the early histories of that time, Léon Poliakov's *Harvest of Hate*, published originally in France in 1951, Grynspan (as it is spelled in his book) is mentioned in two places. In the English translation, Poliakov describes Herschel as "pious, a bit of a mystic, somewhat *exalté*" – hotheaded, fanatical. The assassination, he writes, "came so opportunely for the Nazis that it has been supposed that an agent provocateur armed Grynspan." Herschel was extradited to Germany, and a trial was scheduled for May 1942. It was canceled, writes Poliakov, because "Grynspan had threatened to 'sabotage' the trial by publicly revealing his supposed homosexual relationship with vom Rath."

No mention is made of the fate of Herschel.

The Jews went as sheep. People say that. Here is a Jew who fought back. But is an assassin a fighter? He didn't shoot Hitler. Shot a symbol. An unknown symbol. Made vom Rath famous.

How do you get promoted in the Reich?
Kill Jews. Or get assassinated by one.

Herschel had talked of suicide but did not attempt it. When he was jailed, he fasted once a week in repentance. But he was not humbled. He bragged about what he'd done, wrote to Hitler asking for restitution for the Jewish people. He also wrote letters to other world leaders. His signature became large, full of flourishes.

Herschel's family rallied behind him, even as his aunt and uncle were charged and found guilty of harboring an illegal immigrant.

He made a mess. He killed a quasi-innocent man. An unarmed man. A nice guy, according to those who knew him.

But what, says my friend Marguerite, who is an expert on German literature, if you buy Daniel Goldhagen's argument, that the Germans were willing executioners, that ordinary Germans were responsible for the Holocaust, that there was something in the German psyche that allowed them to pursue the Final Solution – if so, then Herschel did go after the right guy, he went after a heretofore nameless functionary, the ordinary German, the banal cog in the whole system, the one who didn't say no, who went along with the crowd, joined the party because it was the thing to do.

Vom Rath joined the National Socialist Party in 1932. He was along for the ride. He was killed in 1938, before the Wannsee Conference, where the Final Solution was crafted. But still, it's true: vom Rath, dead, had the entire Reich behind him.

J'ACCUSE

In Paris, Herschel's lawyer – Corsican, prominent, paid for by Dorothy Thompson's committee – urged him to claim he had shot vom Rath for personal reasons. Herschel refused. A few years later, after the war had broken out and Herschel was transferred to Germany, he took the lawyer's advice belatedly and claimed a liaison. Vom Rath was especially vulnerable because his brother had been found guilty of homosexual offenses; the brother had been sentenced to a year in prison and had been stripped of his rank as first lieutenant. (The brother died during the war and was rehabilitated after his death.)

Herschel told an investigating psychiatrist in Germany that he had met Ernst vom Rath on the street in Paris, at a newsstand or toilet, and that vom Rath had successfully propositioned him. According to Herschel, vom Rath claimed he was the embassy counselor and could help Herschel's parents. When vom Rath didn't deliver on his promises, Herschel killed him.

Goebbels wrote in his journal that it was a "shameless fabrication" but knew it would be a propaganda nightmare.

The trial was postponed by Hitler, and in effect, canceled.

Herschel disappeared. To this day, no body has been found and identified.

What is the universal law of lost and found? Hide in the place where it's too obvious to look – hide an object in the place where there are many of the same. Hide the tree in the forest, hide the flower in the garden, hide the Jew among the Jews. Among the dead Jews, it appears, not the relatively few who remained alive.

According to Anthony Read and David Fisher in their book *Kristall-nacht: The Unleashing of the Holocaust*, Herschel "almost certainly perished in Sachsenhausen concentration camp at the end of 1942 or the beginning of 1943."

He's also been said to be living in a Paris suburb under an assumed name, married with two children, working in a garage. There was also a report he was a record-store owner in the United States.

Doubtful for many reasons, say Read and Fisher. When they and other researchers followed the rumors to their sources, they found scant evidence. And besides, Read and Fisher say, Herschel saw himself as heroic and would not have stayed hidden. And he was attached to his family and would have sought them out after the war.

In 1960 his father, Sendel, who spent the war in the Soviet Union, applied to the German government for restitution in compensation for his son's death.

He testified at the Eichmann trial. He spoke in German.

THE ROUTE NOT TAKEN

If Herschel had done nothing, most likely he would have been deported – eventually. Sent to Auschwitz. He would not have been a good candidate for hiding underground. When he was released from French prison in the confusion of the 1940 German invasion, he wandered from jail to jail, asking to be imprisoned; he was afraid the Nazis would find and execute him.

In 1936, Gerald Schwab writes, a Czechoslovak journalist shot himself during a meeting of the League of Nations in Geneva in order to protest the Nazi treatment of Jews. "His gesture was promptly forgotten," writes Schwab. In Prague there's a memorial to a student, Jan Palach, who immolated himself in protest after the Prague Spring was crushed. Palach was part of a student-worker coalition and was expressing despair shared by many other citizens. Hundreds of thousands attended his funeral. If you are part of a movement, you are not considered so crazy. In East Berlin, the street leading to the Jewish cemetery is called Herbert Baum-strasse, named for the young Jewish Communist who died in jail after his arrest for setting fire to a propaganda exhibit in 1942. He and members of his political group are also commemorated at the entrance of the cemetery. Their posthumous reputation was helped by the fact that they were Communists in a newly Communist country.

The Jewish Brigade, soldiers from Palestine, trained and fought as part of the British Army from 1944 to 1945, then helped resettle refugees and also sought vengeance. One of them reflected fifty years later in a documentary film, "We proved to the world that we can fight. We proved to ourselves that we could fight."

In the Eastern ghettos, most famously in Warsaw, young people fought off the Nazis, impossibly fought them off in guerilla action as they were starving and sick themselves. In Warsaw they took turns sleeping in different rooms of their hideout, some rooms less desirable than others, all named after concentration camps. They felt alone. Yet even the ones who felt alone wrote of feeling alone together. The remnants of a group in Kraków, the only Jewish fighting group in Kraków, wrote in 1943, "Jews in Palestine will be the only ones to remember us with genuine excitement."

Herbert Baum was a Communist. Herschel attended a club for émigrés that was nominally socialist, but he wasn't political, as far as we know. Herschel. Herbert. Who was the hero? Who was more courageous? If you are impulsive can you not also be courageous? The world does not like loners. Even Joan of Arc had an army behind her.

The Grynszpan family, living in Israel, told the *Jerusalem Post* in

1988 that Herschel was not responsible for the night of broken glass, but was, rather, a freedom fighter. "Crystal Night was Hitler's crime," a daughter of Herschel's brother told the *Post*. "Herschel's act was one of the first expressions of Jewish resistance to the Nazis."

Her sister said it was a shame that "his story is not taught in schools and that he is not held up as a shining example of youthful dedication and self-sacrifice. Herschel is a national hero."

THE HISTORIAN

Of course it would have been better if Herschel had killed Goering or Hitler, a historian tells me, but Herschel did the right thing. He did what he could. There is something to killing a symbol, he says.

The historian is in town to teach two courses at a local university. He was born in Europe to an assimilated Jewish family; his parents died in Auschwitz.

Someone should kill Le Pen, the French right-wing demagogue, the scholar tells me. It would have been better ten years ago, now it is too late, he says. We are sitting in the formal foyer of an apartment-hotel. Soon the room will be used for a university function.

I am too shy to ask him, Why didn't you shoot him?

CHICAGO NOVEMBER

I have moved from one North Side apartment to another. I go to the bank, main branch, for new checks. I see the date on the counter: November 9, 1998. November 9. Kristallnacht. There is repression and caution in here, because it is a bank, because 1997 was a record year for bank robberies in the Chicago area. Even though this is just a neighborhood bank, with a benign-looking security guard whose purpose seems to be to notice when people leave their umbrellas behind. I imagine myself demanding money from the teller. The way part of me wants to yell in a crowded theater, pull a fire alarm, grab a policeman's holster. If my family were deported in another city, would I march into a large stone building, one that feels as official and decorous as this one, my hand heavy with a gun?

I know that, even though we are fellow Ostjuden under the skin, Herschel and I are not the same. I am not oppressed. My family members are full-fledged citizens of the fine state of Texas. I am a property owner. (I bought the new apartment.) I am a member of a mostly non–discriminated against minority (in this country), dealing with my neighborhood bank in my native language. In other places and times, I would be categorized myriad ways, but here and now I am "white." The skin of privilege. I have a right to be in my bank, ordering new checks and asking why the ATM ate my card. Downstairs my savings bonds and computer disks are tucked inside my safe deposit box. Once when I went to put another bond in the box, the man down there told me that there are some people, old people, who come every day, every single day, to check their boxes.

MOVEABLE FEAST

When I went to Paris the first time, in 1976, when I was twenty, it was in order to escape anomie and an oppressive boyfriend. I was enrolled in a French language school for college credit. I was depressed and unfocused. What was I doing there, what was I doing with my life? I thought of cutting myself off from my family, surely the source of my troubles. My parents wrote me kind letters. I cried throughout the city, eating éclairs and big chocolate bars, apple tarts, croissants, baguettes – plain and *complet*, wrote sorrowfully in my journal. Afraid I would not amount to anything. I knew nothing of the French concentration camps of Gurs and Drancy, or of the yellow stars French Jews had been forced to wear. A friend of a friend was Parisian and had a Jewish private last name and a public French last name. I couldn't understand why – where was anti-Semitism? An older couple, cousins of my cousins, invited me one day to lunch, plied me with food and welcome. They had spent the war years in South Texas but we didn't talk about why they left or why they came back. I went to multilingual therapists to pour out the many troubles of my anxious, chronically asthmatic, very lost self. I did not belong in France, but I didn't belong anywhere else, not at my university, not in my hometown. Eventually I made friends, had boyfriends – one American, one Tunisian. I loved the language, hated myself, had nowhere else to go. Heimatlos of the soul.

I had never heard of Herschel then, barely of Kristallnacht.

In Paris in 1976 I began to have a glimmer of world politics. I began to understand that the United States was a superpower and to realize that I had a precious possession, an American passport.

The summer of 1997 was the first time I'd been back to France. I was alone but not depressed. I did research, went to museums, sat in cafés, talked to Israelis and Americans. One day, in the archives of the Jewish documentation center, where I went through files about Herschel's case, a librarian handed out pieces of chocolate. I shared a big wooden table with a Romanian Holocaust survivor and an American French professor who was writing about the Dreyfus case. It was hot and humid and the archives were open only in the afternoon. The staff made photocopies for us and talked loudly. I felt I was in the right place.

DIASPORA

I live in the country I was born in. Any periods of exile have been self-imposed. I speak and write pure American. My father, his father, and his mother are buried in the family plot in Houston. I don't know if I have a place there, but I do know, in the strange grammar of such things, that I have made an anatomical gift – "effective upon my death," it says on the back of my driver's license. I have checked the box that says "entire body."

So I have willed my body to Science – some day my eyes, heart, lungs and liver might be sewn into someone else's body. I think of the blood flowing from the French veteran straight into the dying young German official. (That was how it was done in those days.) Everyone I know asks, What draws you to Herschel? What part of you is he? Is he your alienation? Are you drawn to him because he made a mess? Who is he to you?

He was six months younger than my father. He's someone who could have been my neighbor. He could have been some man in the synagogue on Yom Kippur who spoke in that accent you hear less and less with each passing year. A guy who sold us shoes in my great-uncle's store. He was a kid who fought against the tide of history, which came to him in the concrete form of visa regulations, but originated in the church, in superstition, in poverty. I think what he did was stupid. Frivolous, but not light. For the brief time it took to fire those five shots in 1938, all the weight of history gathered right there in the German embassy in Paris, settling on the slight dark figure who looked a little bit Armenian and had never before used a gun. And the gods laughed.

PLAIN SCARED, OR:
THERE IS NO SUCH THING
AS NEGATIVE SPACE,
THE ART TEACHER SAID

In a college art class I learned that negative space was the nothing behind the figure you were looking at. But years later another teacher told me that this was not so. There is always something there, he said. If you look, you will see it.

Kenophobia is the fear of empty rooms. Fear of empty places. Agoraphobia is the fear of open places. But it is not the agora, the marketplace, that frightens me. I am not afraid to leave the house. I am afraid to leave the city. To be more precise – to venture from the SMSA (Standard Metropolitan Statistical Area).

I live on the North Side of Chicago. I find the word "kenophobia" in a book in the main library of Evanston. About twenty-five years ago, I lived in a dorm room in Evanston. The room was empty when I arrived and empty when I left. I remember one June I kept a university library book almost until the minute the taxi came to take me to the airport. I wanted to keep, as long as possible, some connection with the place I was leaving empty.

I am afraid of being erased. One night in a lover's apartment, after he told me he didn't want to see me anymore, I left this note in his desk: I was here. I was once a part of your life. He has since moved to San Francisco. I do not know what became of the desk.

We are all afraid of being erased. Our names in water writ. Of the earth disappearing. We are small and the night looms.

The night ends. The prairie goes on forever. A sameness, for the uninitiated, the way all the seasons in Miami seem alike to newcomers. I am uninitiated.

We all fear the blank page, the blank mind dry of thought.

In and around Chicago, experts are replanting the prairie. I think this involves both public and private funds. I like reading about such things. I don't mind walking through these prairies if they are small and surrounded by city. It's the big areas I don't like; I don't like to hike. I like to walk through cities, looking in store windows.

I grew up in Texas, came to the Midwest at eighteen. I grew up with ranch houses and sidewalks. In Houston I loved taking the bus downtown and walking among abandoned railroad cars, buying old records in a shabby pawnshop. I'd eat lunch at Woolworth's and buy makeup at Neiman-Marcus.

In my twenties I moved from Illinois to Iowa to Florida back to Illinois. In Iowa I liked the pale green bowls of hills along the highway. I admired them from behind the windows of cars. The hills looked like paintings. In Miami in the newspaper office where I worked, we worshipped the sun from afar. During particularly dramatic sunsets, we reporters would stand near our desks, looking through the windows closest to us, facing west, waiting, watching.

My only forays into nature are very tame – residencies at artists' colonies. I have to pack along piles of little white tablets made of cortisone. When my asthma's bad I take the pills for eight or nine days in a row. I'm allergic to nature. Ragweed, grasses, mold, spores, hay, milkweed – things I can name and things I can't name.

The first artists' colony I went to had once been Edna St. Vincent Millay's retreat a few hours from Manhattan – strawberry farm, hills, pond, trees. At Millay, I learned what foxglove was, and phlox, learned how to spot jack-in-the-pulpit and lady slipper, all veins and sex. The colony's assistant director told me about a New York artist who had come there and had walked around the grounds a while. Then he'd fled inside and reported that he'd seen an animal. What was it? she'd asked. He didn't know. He couldn't tell whether it was a squirrel or a deer.

During my residency, there were two painters who gushed over the landscape. They tried to match the colors of nature with the colors of paint. Cerulean Blue? they would ask each other, pointing at the sky. Havannah Lake?

It is land. It is only land.

The assistant told me that the pioneers from the East feared the flat open land of the West. For some of them, the horizon was too large. They couldn't see themselves in it. They were diminished. Some Easterners returned. Some carved themselves into the Western landscape.

I am not from the East but I understand those Easterners. I don't like limitless horizons. I don't embrace endless fields. I like nature with borders.

The plains scare me.

I am plain scared.

I am terrified of the universe that has no end. I am afraid to step behind the curtain, ask, What is the system behind this solar system? And behind that.

There is no negative space, only positive space having a bad day.

Franz Kafka was born in a city and was buried there. In 1912 he wrote: "Ever since childhood, there have been times when I was almost unhappy about my inability to appreciate flowers. This seems to be related in some way to my inability to appreciate music."

I like flowers. A flowerbed is not the same as a field. Which life depends on. Wildlands are beautiful, they say. They must be saved. There is music in the prairie, they say.

Kafka is less foreign to me than Wendell Berry. I feel closer to Mikhail Zoshchenko's Moscow of the bureaucratic 1920s than Larry McMurtry's Texas.

I find myself inside books by writers who write in fast, urgent sentences with no time for landscape. Writers of closeup conversations – internal and external – writers of the life of streets, cafés, stores, restaurants. Writers who rent. But there are others, so many others; I am not always curled up with my own kind. But I skip the parts, all the parts, about nature.

When I was younger, my friends and I would find books with sex in them. We would read those parts aloud, skip everything else.

Therefore, nature is the opposite of sex.

I know two women in western Michigan who like to read farm novels. One of them has tiny plastic cows and horses super-glued to her dashboard. I don't think I've ever read a farm novel, though I imagine myself finding pleasure in following the slow quiet rhythms of crops pushing their way skyward, in descriptions of the dirt and sweat and dampness of stables, the lowing and groaning. Pure, sweet tiredness after you latch the door, blow out the lantern.

I was in the late Kroch's and Brentano's bookstore on South Wabash Avenue in Chicago. A street with the same name as a river, believed to be taken from the Miami Indian word for "gleaming white." At the bookstore I picked up *A River Runs through It*. Originally a sleeper of a book reissued, glamorized by Hollywood. It is my friend K.'s favorite book. I never talk to K. anymore because he met his ex-girlfriend through me. Somehow that is a problem, though we were never lovers. These are the sorts of things I write about – things that happen indoors. I like K.'s writing, respect his judgment. But I didn't buy the book. I was afraid I would not enter it, afraid of some flatness of surface, nothing to hold onto. Like being afraid to enter into a conversation with a person who has a difficult accent or an unfathomable expression; scratch and scratch and still there may be nothing there.

Or like being afraid of sex, afraid to enter its raw territory, afraid I will find myself in the middle of it, not want to be there, and feel alone, terribly alone, too aware of my surroundings.

§

Many years ago I had an internship in downstate Illinois at the *Quincy Herald-Whig*. I made friends with a young reporter there from a smaller town. She told me, All cities are alike. She didn't see the point in going to more than one of them.

I use free address labels from the Sierra Club and Nature Conservancy. I am not a member. Over the years I've joined the National Trust for Historic Preservation and the Chicago Architecture Foundation. I used to love the before and after spreads in magazines on restored opera houses, movie theaters saved from the wrecking ball and transformed into quaint shopping malls. I loved reading about the resurrection of inner cities, led by young urban pioneers, before "yuppie" was a bad word, or maybe even a word at all.

In Chicago once I met a lawyer who worked for the National

Trust. Soul mate, I thought. She said, I'm really an environmentalist, I don't really have a feeling for architecture. I was appalled. This was hard for me to understand. I told her over and over: You must see the Victorian Gothic apartments at Chicago and Wabash. The building is in danger. It is beautiful. It must be saved.

§

They say you'll see everybody you know if you stand long enough at the corner of State and Madison. I see Louis, that is all that matters. I am talking about a building. I am talking about Carson Pirie Scott, designed by Louis Sullivan. The green and rust filigree ironwork. The design is inspired by organic shapes, the same energy of nature that animated Whitman. This ersatz vegetation fills my heart, the way that Sullivan's first view of a suspension bridge shook him up as a boy. An exhilaration. The same feeling I get from walking down a certain street in my neighborhood, Roscoe – the pedestrian scale of the two-flats and three-flats, the undulation of the brick fronts, the Italianate eyebrows on windows, decorative carvings on graystones – the way *someone* must react to the undulations of corn, clouds, furrows.

Or the straight vastness of the Great Plains with their wheat, earth, sand, clay – whatever is on them, in them.

I liked *Charlotte's Web* – and it appears to have been a farm novel. I fear the Other.

I am afraid nothing is out there but God and landscape, and He doesn't exist and land can't talk. I don't know the language of it.

I like crowded civic and political events during which everyone believes something important is happening.

We city folks go to therapy.

We fantasize about strangers on the El.

We fool ourselves into thinking we have a shared destination.

We fool ourselves into thinking we don't.

§

This is the secret, the secret I have always known: that the bare open plain is my heart itself, my heart without connection; that the bare cinder block room is my soul, my soul without connection – the place I fear I will end up when the fear of loss of connection overrides everything else.

I long to receive this benediction: May you see that something is always there, have hope for the heart to rise up for, come to a feeling of settlement, find a light way of walking on the earth.

Chicago: Loss of Property

$ – The Pickpocket and I

I know him only by his work. A person of action, this pickpocket. Pickpocketeer, pickpocketess. Leaving no traces. Leaving only what he or she did not take: the checkbook, the keys, my work ID. He worked fast. I first notice when I walk onto the El car and swing my knapsack onto the seat and see the open zipper and lack of blue wallet. No wallet. The moment of loss is the same as any moment of denial: No, he couldn't mean that. No, it's not going condo. No, she didn't really die. No, I didn't have my wallet with me. I don't have a wallet, never had a wallet.

In that wallet I had $85, a credit card, a few pictures, postage stamps. A business card on the back of which I'd just copied: And so we came forth, and once again beheld the stars. *E quindi uscimmo a riveder le stelle*. Dante. I could copy the same lines again, from the same magazine article I'd just gotten them from. Everything can be replaced. I didn't even like that wallet. The parrot design had faded after the first week but I'd never bothered to return it. I'd lost it once before and it had come back, intact, though penniless.

Panic. But not the panic of not knowing what to do. The panic growing from the surprise of it: that something like this could happen to me, unawares.

It happened at the Howard Street El station. It is a famous street though there are no books – that I know of – named for it. You make decisions there. It's the end of the line, the northern border of Chicago, a terminus, a beginning and end of bus routes, a beginning for the Skokie Swift, and the Linden El to Evanston and Wilmette. Evanston, formerly dry, is longtime home of the Woman's Christian Temperance Union, whose modest national headquarters is spitting distance from my alma mater, Northwestern University. Evanston is integrated, meaning blacks live south and west and whites live north and especially east, by the lake. Howard is a border street, the first glimpse of the city for the otherwise suburb-and-lake-locked university town. Liquor store on the corner, pawnshop across the street, a pinball parlor nearby. The almost-24-hour Gold Coin coffee shop (Cold Groin to countless Northwestern students). But there's also the softening effect of a flower shop and the promise of renewal: Second Opinion Service for cars.

Poor people live around the stop, many of them black and Latino, therefore making the area "dangerous." Pizza places are said to refuse to deliver nearby. Of course it is the poverty of the people, and not their race, that makes the crime, but we often don't take the time to differentiate. Or to think of the reasons that "minority" and "poor" and "urban" are used interchangeably, or to examine the relation between unemployment and crime, and education and unemployment, and racism and all of them.

Two years ago on a Sunday afternoon a woman approached my friend and me on Howard Street and told us her purse had just been snatched. Years before, waiting in line outside a popular Mexican restaurant off Howard, where, it was said, horse or dog meat had been served in the guise of beef, I saw a fight break out. I'd never seen such a thing in Evanston.

In freshman psychology back in 1975, the professor was telling us about the place in the body that functions as Message Central, where synapses meet and greet. It's like Howard Street, he said. We laughed, in recognition, in pride at how far we had come from our far-flung high schools, joined in our mastery of the once-unknown city transit system, able to make our way to places unknown.

Now I live south of Howard in the city, near Belmont, another important El stop. Important because it's a transfer point. Outside the Belmont station homeless people stand, forming a gauntlet, asking for money. There's a pawnshop across the street – but also three cafés within three blocks where you can order espresso (caf and decaf). There's nice housing, occasional flowerbeds; the area is richer and whiter than near Howard.

$ – 911

I got out of the El car at Howard and reported the missing wallet to uniformed men behind a glass window on the platform. They said to call 911. It was not an emergency so I called from home. I said: I know you won't get me my money back but at least you'll know that somebody was pickpocketed there and maybe if you get more reports, some day you'll send another cop to patrol there. We'll send one now, he said.

$ – 4 A.M.

Phone ringing. Heart throbbing. My father is dead – that's all I can imagine. A voice – male, harsh, strange – says my name. A question. I ask who it is. He doesn't say. He found my wallet. On the El. Which one? Jackson Park line, he says. (It originates at Howard.) We talk about returning the wallet. Somehow we agree to meet on the subway platform downtown at Washington and State at 5 P.M. He has at least three picture IDs to know me by. I say I'll be wearing a gray coat. He says he has a jeans jacket. That's all. He speaks Black English. He sounds black. What does it mean to live in a world where people sound black or white, where there is Black English and Standard English?

I ask him, Why are you calling so late? I probably do not sound grateful. So early? he corrects. He has to leave for work. Where? Franklin Park, a western suburb. In the background I hear a radio or TV and a baby crying.

I suspect a setup, that someone will rob my apartment at 5 P.M. while I'm safely out of the house, waiting at Washington and State. I call the neighborhood police, ask if they'll watch the building. I end up calling cops who ride the rails, a special unit that I later hear advertised on AM radio. It goes something like this (gravel voice): Beware, criminals. We'll no longer put up with rape or robbery or spitting or smoking on the Chicago Transit Authority buses and trains.

They say they'll send three undercover cops to my office downtown. We'll want to talk to this guy, they say.

The head of the unit meets me at my office. He looks like a retired football player. His team comprises a blonde, a huge black man and a white man with crisp light eyes and curly hair. A middle-aged Mod Squad. All in civilian clothes.

I pace the platform at rush hour, plains-clothers watching. I know Chicago is still, unfortunately, segregated, that blacks usually take the southbound trains home, and whites, the north. For the most part.

But I haven't noticed that at this particular stop, they wait on opposite ends of the platform. On which end would he seek me? I stand on one side, walk to the other. It's hard not to laugh from feeling foolish, overdramatic, when you know that four friendly cops are tailing you.

As per our agreement, I am wearing my gray coat. The platform clears and fills, but no one approaches me. After a half hour, the cops tell me: It's a bust. If he calls, be angry. Deny you brought the police.

Police work is a waiting game, they say. They often catch pickpockets in the act, they say. It's rare for the victim to get called like this, they say. We are involved in a mystery together.

I take the El home, without incident.

$ – PHONE

At around 7:30 P.M., the phone rings. It's him. He's sorry, there were a lot of people in gray coats.

I forget to sound angry. There were too many cops, he says. I don't ask: Why should that bother you? As if the answer were understood. As if we were in collusion. He tells me this time he found my wallet on the bus. Not the El.

I tell him he can send it. All day, people have been telling me that you can drop a wallet into any mailbox for free delivery but I feel protective, don't want my wallet to go through more strange hands. I tell him he could send it in a padded envelope. He says he doesn't know how to get one. For a moment he sounds almost ready to mail it, says if I wanted I could send a reward. I say I would. He backs down, says he wants to meet. I suggest Carson Pirie Scott department store. He counters: the Burger King at the bus station, 5 P.M. I ask what he looks like. He says he's six-foot-two, 155 pounds. What else? I ask, groping. Do you have a beard? He says slowly, Yes, a long beard. It sounds untrue. As unlikely as his weight. I ask his name. He says why do you need to know that? I say, so I can be sure it's you. Joe, he says.

Then the phone rings again. I answer and someone hangs up. It rings again, keeps on ringing. I don't want to be alone with the ringing phone. I go downstairs, knock on two neighbors' doors. From the hall I can still hear the phone. I imagine calling 911 to report a fiercely ringing telephone. No one answers at either neighbor's. I return, pick up the phone. It's an acquaintance. He say he was waiting for the answering machine to kick in. I wonder when he would have given up – at 50 rings? 75? 200?

$ – FRIENDS

My friend Jennifer advises me to bail out. Says it's dangerous. I feel guilty for playing with such fire. In the morning the cops at the Neighborhood Watch at the end of the block say the same thing, that the guy is playing with me, will never show up.

I call the undercovers. They are surprised he called. Nearly delighted. We agree to meet downtown on a street corner.

I talk to my friend Jessica. Of course it's exciting, she says. She's going to the Burger King to watch. You should call everybody, she says. It's performance art.

I stand on the designated corner. Full of shoppers. Then one of the Mod Squad is just sort of there. Has glided in beside me. It is balletic. Across the street are the other two, the leader, and reinforcements. They tell me to remove my scarf when I get the wallet. I tell them I may give him a reward. He may even deserve one. What if, indeed, he did find my wallet and is going out of his way to return it?

Your decision, the police say.

At Burger King I take a window seat, so the cops who are stationed outside can see me. I eat my salad and try to read a magazine. Jessica walks in. I shake my head slightly, afraid the cops will note this and think we're somehow in collusion, engineering an elaborate double cross. She takes a seat across the room.

Two of the Mod Squad are at nearby tables, the others, outside. Around a quarter after five, a man comes to my table. He's black, tall, maybe something like six-two. He's thin, maybe something like 145. He has a trim beard. Says something like: Are you the lady here for the wallet?

I reach for it, forget to take off my scarf.

Immediately he's surrounded, a gun to his ribs. I move to the side to disassociate myself. Can't look him in the eye. But what did I expect? I did summon the police, after all.

They question him. He says he works in Franklin Park, says he was just returning the wallet. I find out his name is not really Joe. They search him and find plastic: a couple of supermarket check cards, a senior citizen discount card. My U.S. Sprint calling card. I'd forgotten about that, hadn't thought of calling the company to cancel it.

I have lost $85 and I'm the one who feels guilty. Perhaps this is a good Samaritan before me, handcuffed, caught in a police sting? A dumb Samaritan, perhaps, who doesn't know better than to call someone at four in the morning and can't figure out how to get hold of a padded envelope?

$ – THE COP SHOP

Police headquarters is at 11th and State, a mile and a half south, dingy, busy, but not frantic. Jessica and I get a ride.

We wait at a table and are joined by another victim, a man who's all shook up and voluble. I don't care, he says, what color a man is, white, black, yellow. Nobody can take my hard-earned money. The man speaking is black; so is the man who robbed him, he says.

This, I know, is one of the more common pairings – blacks committing crimes against blacks, whites against whites. The man tells us he was robbed on the El on the way home from work in a nursing home. He says something like this: I don't care who he is, he had no right to put a gun to me. He lambastes the conductor for not watching out for passengers. The man had kicked or hit the muggers, knocking away a gun. He is here to identify the perpetrators. I'm a black belt in karate, he says. He was in the Marines for six years.

Meanwhile, cop life goes on around us. One says into a phone: I love you. This sets off serious teasing. It's my brother, he says. You're a sick guy, someone says. They joke with each other about ex-wives. Behind the main desk, in a large cage – there is no other word for it – are skinny black kids, looking scared. I wonder if they'd be held like that, or even picked up, if they were white. Jessica tells a policeman she's appalled. He says, Probably turnstile jumpers, waiting for their mothers to pick them up.

Then I make a statement, get a court date. They find out that the 911 cops didn't even make a report when I called.

I ask the Mod Squad sergeant: What about rehabilitation? Is that possible?

No, he says. Rehabilitation, he repeats, it's a good word to read.

He says this guy could get up to a year, for possession of stolen prop-erty and for deception – not returning it promptly. Could. He says it depends on the judge's mood.

One of the cops who's questioned the man says that "Joe" claimed he found the credit cards. He tells us: I've been riding on the subway three years and never found any.

If he was the pickpocket, why did he call me, aside from hopes for a small reward?

Pickpockets are dumb, says the sergeant. Burglars are the smart ones.

I tell them I'm afraid that "Joe" will try to get revenge. The cops predict that he won't bother me.

$ – IN COURT

The judge calls about forty names, one after the other, for the stating of charges and the murmurings of the public defender and assistant state's attorneys. The charges, from what I can hear: turnstile jump-ing, disorderly behavior, shoplifting at Lord & Taylor, assault. Most of the defendants are black men. They look elated or blank after the sentence. A number of the sentences – the ones I can hear – seem to be probation.

"Joe" arrives late. He's wearing a black down jacket, and a mild ex-pression. Like so many of the others, when he stands before the judge, he holds his hands behind his back, as if already handcuffed. He says he makes $10 an hour as a machinist, pays $475 a month rent. He won't settle for the offered three months court supervision. He wants a trial. So we will have one. April 30.

In the hallways, the Mod Squad blonde says: When you go back in, look at that young guy on the back row. She describes his jacket. If you see him on the El, get away. He'll fight you for your wallet.

I ask why he's not in jail.

He's good, she says. Hard to catch.

My wallet-returner has left the courtroom ahead of me. I see him downstairs by the vending machines. I slink away.

Later he's declared not guilty. Case closed. I never hear from him again.

AT THE ROSE OF SHARON
SPIRITUAL CHURCH

Chicago's first African American mayor, Harold Washington, died in 1987 of a heart attack during his second term. The alderman chosen as acting mayor was Eugene Sawyer, also black. In 1988 one of Sawyer's (black) assistants, Steve Cokely, was widely reported to have given incendiary sermons in Louis Farrakhan's church. Local newspapers said that among other remarks, Cokely claimed that Jewish doctors were injecting black children with AIDS. Under pressure, the mayor fired Cokely. Cokely's supporters rallied around him. Just after the dismissal, some friends of mine in the media – all of us white – drove to Chicago's West Side, a mostly black, mostly poor area of town, to observe a rally in support of Cokely.

It is dusk. I have never been to the West Side before. I have been through it, past it, once or twice, and one time pointed out a few sights from a window on an architectural tour. This is a "bad" neighborhood, a poor black neighborhood – empty storefronts, bad schools. Danger. I live north and east, in a mixed but mostly white area: well-kept apartments, cafés, occasional gang graffiti, bad schools. I was driven here by Ann, a journalist, a friend of my friend Bill's, a photographer who follows controversy. Andy, another journalist, sits in front. This is history, news. We are recorders of the news – curious, white. The other three have followed the story for days – press conferences in City Hall, denials, accusations, finally, the firing. Ann's an editor, Bill takes pictures, Andy covers the Midwest for an Eastern newspaper. I write stories, poems, and articles. I freelance. I take rides when they're offered. Andy and I are Jewish. We met on Yom Kippur, the Day of Atonement, in South Florida, five years ago.

There are other journalists here. They are white. The people to be observed are black. They are angry.

Outside the church, before the speeches begin, a man tells me he is a Hebrew, a universalist, not Jewish, that like Joseph in the Bible, he is black, that blacks are the true Hebrews described in the Bible – despised, downtrodden. He points to his dark skin, to the skin of the other dark men around him. This is the meaning, he says, of Joseph's coat of many colors. He says, Jonah was black, too.

I don't care. I don't believe in Joseph and Jonah as historical figures; they are metaphors. I say, The god of the Bible is too hard for me to accept. Patriarchal. I declare my disbelief, to this stranger who asks if I consider myself to be Greek. Greek? He tells me about the Greek translation of the Bible, concludes something from this that I can't follow. Am I Greek or not? He pushes me to declare. What are my origins? Pressed, I say, Eastern Europe. I don't tell about my absurd nostalgia for the Moldavian city, Kishinev, that my family left two generations ago. But I am not East European. I am American, North American, a *norteamericana* who has learned how dangerous words can be. I have learned that Zionism has become a dirty word. Two decades ago, in childhood, it was naive, plain, boring, as in: Zionist youth group. Eretz Tzion. The land of Zion. But even then, holding the memory of an ugly threat: *The Protocols of the Elders of Zion*. A hoax of a book, popularized by Henry Ford, among others. Some Jews won't buy Fords, still. Mistrust burned into us.

When I go inside to sit down, the man next to me says, I can't sit here, and moves up a row. He can't sit next to me. What have I done to *him*? But what has the black man done to me, the black stranger that makes me flinch as I walk at dusk in Rogers Park on the Far North Side? We have made each other monsters. Or symbols. My skin means power.

And I know whites who flinch under the hands of black doctors, who won't vote for blacks (avoiding all names that sound like early presidents: Washington, Jefferson, Madison). I know whites – Jews, one particular Jew, an elderly cousin, actually – who trust no outsiders. This is nature's law, according to my cousin: The Gentile will say he's your friend, but you can't count on him.

I know white Christians who say worse.

I know all kinds who work their whole lives as bridges.

Not many.

A man three rows behind me cries out: Jew busters, Jew busters! What does that mean? I want to turn to him, to offer myself, as challenge or maybe sacrifice, to say, What will you do to me? Here I am, the vilified, horned Jew. As I have been for centuries. I want to offer myself, to shame him, them, because he would do nothing, now. It is not dangerous here. There is a crowd, media, witnesses.

At the altar, a man in a purple print shirt recites the Shema. His style is rough reggae staccato. He's saying it wrong, his foreign stresses rendering it all but unrecognizable. This man calls himself a black Hebrew. I know the Shema of the Diaspora, North American–accented. He could be saying it the way the Sephardic Jews say it, for all I know. His accent could be Israeli. But I doubt it.

He is angry. The people here are angry. *Jew busters, Jew busters*. At the altar now the Rev. Al Sampson is disparaging our 6 million. He says that we disparage their 125 million who died as slaves. Later I hear that a better estimate is somewhere between 30 and 100 million. A man in the audience disputes that 6 million Jews died in Hitler's camps.

How do you compare destruction?

Steve Cokely is speaking now. He says: We never did anything to you.

From the audience: Yet, yet.

What have I done?

So easy to be the innocent, so easy to say, During your four hundred years of slavery, we were living across the ocean, studying, trading, fleeing our own persecutors. It is not our fault. Are my hands bloody?

And they could answer: But your whole life you have benefited from your white privilege.

And then? And then? Should I dedicate my life to seeking economic justice and freedom, to reaching across barriers? I do that a little, could do more. But what to do about these people here who are not my enemies, who send forth conspiracy theories constructed of wind and loose threads, conspiracy theorists who point fingers at me, at my people?

The man outside told me, I don't know my great-great-grandfather. He said, You probably know yours or you could ask your parents. Almost as an accusation. Almost as if to show me: See how deracinated we are.

My mother knows of her grandfather who was a blacksmith. I have

relatives with charts that lead back to Ireland and Spain. On my father's mother's side, I could get names, dates. My father knows whom
he was named for – his grandfather – knows the date of his death.
That's all. Dead end on my father's father's side, beyond two previous
generations. We do know that they were lucky, they lived through the
famous, brutal Kishinev pogrom of 1903.

The attacks come from the altar: names of Jews, hurled, as if being
Jewish is an indictment. Proof of power, inordinate and preemptive.
Prove someone is Jewish, and that's all you have to do. Because that
in itself is bad. Because Jew equals Israel equals South Africa. Therefore we are all racist, we are in control – watch out. I have read of Israeli cooperation with racist South Africa, rumors of nuclear sharing.
I have read an essay that named three pariah states: Israel, South Africa, Taiwan. Strange ménage. I acknowledge Israel's maltreatment of
Palestinians but would not call it apartheid. American Jews do not
equal Israel. American Jews are American Jews. Varied though not
numerous.

Meanwhile, the cameras are recording. A newscaster winds up his
report on tonight's speechifying and outrage, pronouncing: But it
doesn't stop the problem.

What is the problem? Steve Cokely?

The problem is the unfairness of history. Says a highly excitable
man, as lights shine and film turns: You mistreated us four hundred
years and you want *us* to apologize –

Both are true. They were mistreated and we want them to apologize. If you were mistreated for four hundred years, then can you
say whatever you want? Because we were mistreated for thousands
of years, can New York Mayor Ed Koch say what he wants; because
there are 2 million Jews in New York City, can Koch say it is only a
crazy Jew who would vote for Jesse Jackson?

The problem is the unfairness of the present. The problem is too
big to say simply.

The people in this room are afraid and angry. The activist Marion
Stamps says, If we don't stand up with Steve tonight, they're going to
attack us. Sampson says: If they come for Steve tonight, it will be you
and you and you tomorrow night, Lu Palmer by midnight . . . Farrakhan early in the morning.

The rhetoric reminds me of the famous quote by the minister Martin Niemöller, who said that when the Nazis came for the communists, he didn't speak up because he wasn't a communist, and when they came for the trade unionists and the Jews and the Catholics, he didn't speak up, and by the time they came for him, there was nobody left to speak up.

But the people taken away in Germany were not just fired from city jobs. They were killed.

Cokely says, They want us to look fanatical, kooky. He says, I was too powerful in government. And don't think they didn't know it.

But he was not fired because he was powerful. He was fired for what he spread. This is what the papers say: This man said that Jews were conspiring internationally. He said Jews were inoculating black children with AIDS. He said public schools were dangerous. At the Rose of Sharon he tells us that whites took words he spoke to the people of his "house" and took the information to their "house" – to hurt him.

There is so much hate swirling about the room. *Jew busters! Jew busters!* They challenge Jews to a debate. About what? About our innocence? We are innocent. We shouldn't have to prove it. They feel innocent, too. We both feel wounded.

In the car, my friend Bill asks, Did you feel threatened?

No. Is this how Jews felt in Germany fifty-five years ago, unable to imagine that anyone could harm them? I feel foolish, alarmist. This is America, not Germany. And yet, they are preaching the same hatred. But to call them Nazis would be fanning the flames. Of the fire they started. I am not part of a conspiracy.

After his brothers sold him, Joseph became a famous man in Egypt, governor appointed by the king. When there was a famine in Israel, his family came to join him. Joseph's people became numerous and strong. They had their own customs. The Pharaoh decided they had to be watched, controlled, enslaved. I know this story by heart. This is the story of my people, if I choose to believe it. According to the man outside the church, the people in question were blacks, not Jews. If this were proven scientifically, would it make a difference to me? I don't think so.

Did you feel threatened?

No, because of the media, I say. Cameras make things safe. Relatively, not always. And white men. Feminists would point out that I am under the protection of white men. It is true. I am weak. Though I have been trained in nonviolent civil disobedience. I am a karate class dropout.

Did I feel threatened? No, not personally. And I feel safe enough now, in the car, going east to the Loop. We are out of earshot, the small, intense crowd left behind, the ghetto, out of the way. Did I feel threatened? No. But though I have seen no blood, no riot, no mob, no burning, no swastika – the lights of the city tonight seem especially fragile, especially small.

A few weeks later, I'm in City Hall and see a man standing at the foot of the stairs, talking to a small group. He is familiar – bow tie, striped shirt, suit. Cokely. If there were other members of the press I would take out my notebook, melt into a crowd of listeners. But these are obviously cohorts. Laughing, together. Upstairs, no one in the press room cares. Old news.

An hour later, as I'm leaving, he's still there. I want to say, Hello, I've written about you. Hello, I'm Jewish. Hello, what do you want of me?

Is it a challenge I want to deliver, to show him up morally? Do I want to hold out my hands, so he will see that they are not the hands of an imperialist?

But I say nothing, and go on to the rest of my errands downtown – stop at the office, the cash machine – not declaring my innocence, not delivering a challenge, not extending a hand, not making a greeting of any kind.

MEXICO ON $15 A DAY

The Feminist Writers Guild was collecting books for Cook County Jail. The newsletter announced it. I called my friend Joyce for more information. I asked, What kind? The warden had told her, Any book is fine, long as it's paperback. Proud she was not censoring. The county jail did not have a proper library, women's side. The guild had plans to fill it with donations. We speculated: Hardbound, perhaps, could be made into weapons. Anything is fine, we said, to our own amusement, as long as it's not *How to Bake a File into a Cake, How to Escape Cook County Jail.* Or *The Anarchist Cookbook.* Or *Steal This Book.*

I collect from friends. I walk over to A. and C.'s. We stand in front of the shelves. *Mexico on $15 a Day*? A. asks. It is paperback. The prices are outdated. Is it better to have dreams of impossible destinations? I ask. Or is it better not to know that people vacationed in Mexico on $15 a day? Will three inmates be found on the bus to Juarez, clutching Frommer's like a promise? Will they turn themselves in, disillusioned by the out-of-date prices, will they be caught shoplifting in Matamoros, rot in a Mexican jail, deprived of rights, longing for the three square meals at Cook County?

C. reminds him, edges of her lips turning down: Pack the shelves. What she means is to make sure the books are packed tightly in, when he's through taking out the ones to give away. Otherwise, their toddler will pull them out. She has done it before. Before the baby, two years ago, they went to Mexico, came back and showed slides of monarch butterflies that had glided to their hands, faces, that gathered on trees. Huge brown flowers. A tribe. Driven by instinct. They showed the slides in the dark. The viceroy mimics the monarch. Did they know that? Were the viceroys lurking among the flock, outsiders finding refuge? Deception was not the point. The point was to wake up for a truck ride to the place of early morning mist, where monarchs lost their fear, where they alighted, weary, protected by sheer numbers. Trusting. Because this was their place of rest. And the ones who gathered to watch in awe, who hired trucks, left them in safety. They were not collectors.

Which is better? To hold the maps in your hand, the escape route out of reach? Or avert your eyes?

Five years before A. met C., he and I were lovers. All I remember, he tells me, is lots of hair. I remember drinking. Dissonance of our rhythms. Months later, still weeping, because I was still alone, I streamed back to him for comfort. He told me: A guy won't make it better. Would not solve it. Could not light my escape. He left, back to his ex-wife, left again, moved, married, made this child. Who pulls at books. Chuckling at her mastery. When we were lovers, we lived in Miami, land of exiles. For my birthday he bought me a guidebook to the region. We never went away for a weekend. We witnessed the aftereffects of migration: no monarchs at rest. Tens of thousands seeking comfort in the re-creation of the familiar. White stucco houses. Café cubano. Goat on the grill. Statues of saints. Drinks made from fruits we'd never seen whole. Reggae. The jumpy edges of the language of Creole. Yiddish-peppered memories of life in the needle trades.

At Cook County Jail the detainees stay too long. Justice creaks. The crimes: Fraud. Prostitution. Possession. Assault. Homicide. Crimes of passion, desperation, deception. *Lots of hair*, he says. What I remember: Champagne – once. Red roses in a vase by the bed. Weeping. His alarm clock, whose set time never varied. His placid unsnapping of the rubber band around the newspapers that arrived each morning. Juice, coffee, bagels. He'd unfold the out-of-state papers, complaining: Why can't somebody down here write like this? Most days he jogged.

Something was coiled within him, deep, waiting to loosen. I couldn't loosen it. I couldn't reach in deeply enough. I was unloosened: my hair, my clothes, my sorrows. Pack the shelves, says his wife. So they won't come undone. They put the paperbacks into shopping bags. Later I haul them out.

The books will be taken downtown, fill the hearts of strangers.

VACATION AT CLUB DEAD

My friend Angie and I had come to Central America to look for truth, the way others (we thought) went there to tramp through Mayan ruins and bargain their way to cheap bright textiles. We were reporters but it wasn't our beat. It was vacation. Club Dead, I called it.

What I knew about Central America had come from the media and from leftish conferences. I believed in the Sandinistas. It mattered, in a way I strain now to recall, that there had been a place governed by a dictator and that the people had arisen, conquered him, and were making a better life. The Nicaraguan revolution was one of the few events of the late twentieth century that showed that improvement was possible, that the world didn't have to remain miserable and poor.

I felt a sympathy with the armed El Salvadoran rebels even though for years I had pronounced myself a pacifist. I asked myself if I would still espouse nonviolence if I lived in Central America. What if my daily life were so brutal that mere survival required violence? And if that sort of violence was justified, wasn't it just one more step to accepting self-defense in all forms, and then revenge, and so on, all the way to the electric chair and the neutron bomb?

It was November 1984. Managua was full of people like us – sympathizers from all over the world, come to watch the first elections since the 1979 revolution. Our tour met with government leaders and some from the nonmilitary opposition. We were taken around in buses and stayed in the ranch-style homes of former Somoza functionaries. Our beds were made and laundry was washed by maids who called us *compañera*, comrade, and wanted to come to America.

In the embattled northern city of Estelí, we walked into tiny schoolroom polling places and through the streets. We talked to women who used to be maids, who used to be scared, whose pictures I took as they pointed to an outdoor mural depicting the people's insurrection. They assured us their elections were fair, and they couldn't understand how the American people could vote for Reagan again.

One day I took a cab to visit parents of a friend of mine, south of Managua. They were landowners. They thought their maid was spying on them. They believed the Contra radio and the articles in *La Prensa*, the anti-Sandinista newspaper stacked on the living room floor. They had pastel toilet paper in the bathroom and I wondered if it was special for me. I knew there was a toilet paper shortage. An aspirin shortage. There was an everything shortage and I felt ashamed I hadn't brought them Band-aids and over-the-counter drugs. They fed me lunch and gave me candy and coffee to take back to their son. They apologized for not being able to drive me back to Managua. Gasoline rationing, they sighed. Only the birds are free, said my friend's aunt.

This was their home. They were waiting for it to seem like theirs again.

I wanted to tell them the Sandinistas were bringing democracy. I wanted to speak of land reform and health care, of cooperation and the redistribution of wealth. I could not refute the truth of their lives. I could not tell them they deserved what they'd gotten, that revolutions are not fought for the benefit of landowners. I could not argue with their son, who had rushed home from college in America to work in the postrevolutionary literacy campaign. Propaganda, he said later, bitterly, and flew back to Missouri.

There is no way to respond to someone who feels betrayed. I returned to my group in Managua, in a government building guarded by a preteenager in olive drab, gun thrust in his waistband. The group was listening to Dora Maria Tellez, "Commander Two," when the National Palace was overtaken. She was still dressed as a soldier.

I am twenty-eight years old, she said. It is Saturday night. I would love to be wearing other clothes and be out with my friends. But I have to protect the revolution.

American helicopters had been threatening the capital. I'd met people a few days earlier who'd said they'd slept flat on the floor, anticipating an attack. Tellez was realistic, eloquent, reassuring. The aims of the revolution were equality and an end to tyranny; she wanted peace and prosperity, a life that was whole. I wanted to cry for her splendor and sincerity and vision.

But compañera Dora, I asked silently, why do your words remind me of the soldier I met while I was protesting at the Pentagon, who answered my objection to killing by saying, as if explaining to a slow child, You can't have a war without killing people?

§

A few days later Angie and I were in San Salvador at the home of a newspaper correspondent. It was a bright, airy place, stark as a Shaker house, barely occupied. His maid took the bus with us to the central marketplace. We walked through the stalls, buying wrapping paper, a plastic mesh bag, figurines, feeling guilty for bargaining. There were mounds of American-brand toothpaste and soap, just more commodities like the bushels of garlic and piles of dusty candy.

We sat down in a bakery. Three young women in their twenties, Angie commented later, shopping and getting coffee and dessert. The maid told us she had a six-year-old son who lived with her parents in her village. They'd been apart since her husband had been killed – by the rebels. The guerillas. The good guys. We expressed sympathy. Of course. We felt sympathy.

The next day Angie and I went to a refugee camp. We saw old men, women, children. Poor children, naked children, standing patiently in line, kids out of Dickens, girls with caps covering their hair, patiently flattening tortillas and cooking eggs. Ringing the camp were guards and cameras. Old women bathed in the open, breasts hanging. Water was rationed. A young woman told us we must tell everyone what we saw. I can't leave, she said, because people would ask where I'm from. She would have to tell about the massacre in her village, the one in which government soldiers killed her husband and son.

Boys were playing some sort of homemade game with nails stuck into a board painted sky blue. Plants grew in large dirt-filled food tins. Women nursed their infants amid flies. I thought: This will continue after we leave and have forgotten about it.

Back at the correspondent's home we took showers. The water was cold. We thought of the maid. We wondered if her husband had been a government soldier. I said, How can we judge? It's not our life. How can we judge, we who have always had hot showers? And, Angie added, who have a lifetime of hot showers ahead of us.

The next day we found out: If you leave the water running long enough, it gets hot.

That day the highway filled with soldiers in trucks leaving the city. They looked very young.

Yizkor (Memorial Service)

for Ben Linder,
the U.S. engineer killed by the Contras in Nicaragua, April 27, 1987

1. Interview with His Parents, Elisabeth and David Linder, on a Speaking Tour Stop in Chicago, September 1987

Elisabeth was small and had nearly the same birth date as my
mother. But so much has happened to her. A lilt in her voice that
turned out to be Czech. David was tall, I asked his height. He
reminded me of an old German woodcarver: white hair, deep-set
eyes, growing deeper by the minute. Knobby hands that looked
made for making things. He was tall – I asked his height. This is
what I do – ask height. Gather numbers. Distances in kilometers,
translated into miles, definitions: "What exactly is a weir?" That is
what Ben was working on, a weir. Something by a stream. Damlike.
His mother knew. Would my mother be able to say why I wrote in
fragments? Could my father tell the difference between prose and a
prose poem? Some things are not analogous. Ben Linder finished a
small hydroelectric plant in a place called El Cuá, in northern Nicaragua. The town has lights now – for night classes. Refrigeration –
for the storage of vaccines.

His parents went down for his funeral. Met with President Ortega,
sat next to Ortega's wife on a bus. She impressed the father. The cabi-
net ministers impressed him too. So down to earth. Poets.
   The procession was seven blocks long.

She was small and had the same birthday as my mother. Nearly.
A week older. His hair was white. Their son was small, so small
the Contras thought he was Cuban. Or so they said. "As if it's
open season on Cubans?" asked the mother. As if a Cuban isn't
somebody's son? But Cuban mothers don't appear before the U.S.
Congress, with the grand *j'accuse:* We hold you accountable for killing our son, for aiding the Contras, the merchants of death that

bomb clinics and destroy weirs, that shoot a son. A Congressman accused her: "Your emotionalism, Mrs. Linder, is blinding you to the truth."

(The truth. The voices of the State Department, when I call to interview them, are so cold, and tell me: "In spite of our warnings, the Nicaraguan government let Benjamin Linder go into a war zone." President Reagan made it a war zone. Congress made it a war zone. Ben was building a weir.)

The parents tour Chicago, the rest of the country, showing slides of their son: Ben on his unicycle. Ben in a polka-dot clown suit. Ben playing Pied Piper so the kids would follow him to get their immunizations. Playing a guitar. Sitting in the house of the old man who gave him a pallet to sleep on. Juggling. These people had a son who juggled. And now they sit, voices quavering at the applause in a church on Chicago's North Side where they speak of their son to the crowd that came to hear them speak of their son. The applause so warm. I sit in a pew near the front and hold my lover's hand. Feel guilty for my joy among the sorrows. *Dr. Linder Mrs. Linder I am in love. I am sorry.*

But they laugh. I heard them, the day before, nearly raucous in the hallway at the public radio station. They were waiting to be interviewed, live. They were so noisy that someone came out to quiet them. Mrs. Linder – Elisabeth – protested: "But we're funny."

But we're funny – write that down. Poignant. "But we're funny."

But Mrs. Lincoln, aside from that, how did you like the play? This edge of horror, this intimate peeling back.

Journalistic license: "So I read he had red hair, is that true? Is it true he was always handy? Is it true he wore a uniform and carried a gun? Was it true you told him he wouldn't make money as an engineer unless he worked for the merchants of death – the companies that contract with the Department of Defense? Are you observant Jews?"

Elisabeth's family escaped the Nazis. They emigrated to Mexico. That's how she knows Spanish.

She's worked as a court translator, gave an interview in Chicago to the Spanish-speaking TV reporters. He says he's an atheist, speaks in a Brooklyn accent. A retired child pathologist. The one who's on call to arrive after untimely deaths. For months the whole family has been on tour, brother with sister starting out in Miami, mother alone, then joined by the father. The brother is some kind of radical. Socialist Worker. Do I mention it? If not, am I guilty – covering up, making the Linders less controversial?

2. THE BODY

He has changed from a son into a body. "Will they exhume the body?" I ask the lawyer by phone. They are waiting. "Will the Nicaraguan government give permission?" A pathologist, famous, working for free, who studies assassinations, says: "It appears close range."

The Contras told the *New York Times*: "We thought he was Cuban."

3. LESSONS

It is open season on Cubans. Not to mention Nicaraguans.

It is subversive to make electricity.

Even if your death is reported in the *New York Times* and your family goes on national tour most people will not have heard of you.

The people who have heard will give money to hear more. They will call you hero and redouble their commitment.

It is possible to laugh afterwards, even after your heart is torn out.

4. YIZKOR

"I shall die," Edna St. Vincent Millay wrote, "but that is all that I shall do for Death; I am not on his pay-roll."

I am not on God's payroll. I am not on death's payroll. My taxes have paid the Contras' payroll. "Because he did not live on the CIA payroll," Ortega said at the funeral, "they killed him."

God, forgive us, as we forgive you, and those who fight in your name.

God, we cannot praise you for all your handiwork.

In my High Holiday prayer book, there is a section in memory of ten martyrs who were crushed in their revolt against Rome, more than nineteen hundred years ago. They were rabbis. There is a list of their names. The book says there were thousands of others. In libraries now you can find Yizkor books that contain names of people killed by the Nazis. Each book is from a different town, written by survivors. Even now, they are still being translated into English. Even now, there are destroyed towns without memorial books.

It is easy to forget that non-Jews are murdered, too, en masse.

My prayer book tells me: "Even the seraphim in the heights of heaven called out in anguish."

My prayer book tells me: God answered them, "The way to truth and justice is often filled with affliction and pain."

From the translated Yizkor prayer:

> *Man is a breath*
> *man is a shadow, frail, short, fleeting*
> *life is not futile, hearts should not despair.*

"I am an atheist," said David Linder. "My son knew the frailty of human flesh." At the funeral in Matagalpa, American Jews recited the Kaddish.

When we feed the hungry, says my prayer book, when we strive for justice, we become immortal, timeless.

"I am an atheist," said David Linder, "yet I believe in a resurrection, the struggle." The struggle continues. *La lucha*. His son's life fueled it.

"We escaped the Nazis," said Elisabeth Linder. "We are funny," said Elisabeth. In the hallway of the public radio station, they laughed.

"It was not an empty death," said David Linder. "At some point my son said there is nothing to do but go forward."

"He had three good years," said Elisabeth. He found his mission. He made electricity.

I am glad I did not die at twenty-seven.

Make us live, we say, make us live forever.

In wet concrete near a stream near San José de Bocay, those who worked with him wrote: "Aquí murió Benjamín Linder, su obra seguirá." Benjamin Linder died here, his work will continue.

We pray: Write us in the Book of Life.

Despair, said the great Rabbi Baal Shem Tov, is the book of death.

We beseech. By the lights that we pray never go out, not quite believing in them or anything else, because of habit/fear/hope/memory, most of all memory, we pray.

THE CHILDREN OF
THERESIENSTADT

If you had been in Theresienstadt, a thirty-minute drive from Prague, on May 29, 1992, you would have seen them: five men in matching T-shirts, and one in a short-sleeved sport shirt. They had been imprisoned there fifty years before and had vowed, One day in fifty years we're going to meet here again and have lunch. And they did.

Theresienstadt was a model camp, emphasis on model, emphasis on camp. Children were divided into groups, like cabins or bunks in a real camp, like those that postwar Jewish-American children lived in for a few weeks each summer. These men, when they were boys, were in a group of nine who lived in such a home permanently away from home. They had a *madrich*, which is Hebrew for "leader." He was in his early twenties. Each group had a team and uniform. They lived together until four were deported to Auschwitz-Birkenau. One of the four was bar mitzvahed at Auschwitz.

In late spring 1992 the men came back to Theresienstadt with families and cameras. And white T-shirts that said, "Rim rim rim tempo nasarim!" It was their motto when they played sports – "the football cry," said one of them, in some kind of European accent, the kind you get from having lived through World War II as a Jew.

Theresienstadt, in German, or Terezín, in Czech, was a collection point for other camps. It was also a showplace, the city Hitler granted to the Jews, as it was called in a propaganda film. It was an exemplary ghetto, or camp, if you were an inspector from the Red Cross. If you lived there, it was not. The tourist's guidesheet points out the place of execution, where 250 people – after being taken first through the Gate of Death – were shot. The largest mass execution was in 1945, when 52 people were killed. Most of them were members of a youth resistance organization.

Others died "natural" deaths; of 15,000 children who passed through the camp, perhaps only 100 survived. In Theresienstadt children starved and died of typhus. And played soccer in the sunshine.

§

If you had been in Theresienstadt that warm Friday in 1992, you would have seen a group of Jewish Americans, all born after the war, loosely connected by old and new friendship. One of them was an official of the American Holocaust remembrance empire on a busman's holiday – having just finished escorting a group of survivors and family members to camps throughout Europe to collect bones and ashes for burial in the U.S. It is a mitzvah, he said, a good deed, to bury the dead. He was vigorous, enthusiastic, like a *tummler* – the social organizer in the Catskills. In the group also was a doctor from Philadelphia. The tummler remarked that German Jews paid for first-class, second-class, and steerage tickets on their way to the east, to where they thought they were going, "hard labor camps." The doctor from Philadelphia said, "My grandfather went to Dachau in top hat and tails."

§

The group of Jewish Americans arcs around the group of former boys of Theresienstadt. The madrich, who now lives in L.A., stands in white T-shirt and dark pants. "He created our personalities," says one of the former boys. The madrich tells the younger Americans about the talk of lunch, half a century ago. His tone is light. He adds, "To me, while I make jokes, this is a horrible moment."

He looks around. "If you didn't have eyewitnesses, you'd think it was an anecdote."

His wife is with him. She lived here in Theresienstadt almost three years. She arrived at age nineteen in 1941, the day after she married her first husband. The Germans promised the couple they would be sent away together.

"We were separated immediately. We should have known. They weren't doing it for love."

She laughs.

She volunteered to open a new camp. When she arrived she looked at the poor people in striped uniforms. "I was not aware I would be one of them."

She found out after the war that her husband had died at Mauthausen.

While she talks, she smiles. She digs her bright red fingernails into her palms. During the war she worked making propellers for aircraft.

"SHEMA, THE FIRST PRAYER YOU LEARN":
Among those I prayed for were my sister Rosi
(*left*) and Greg the Dachshund. I am on the
right. This is 1961, Fairhope Street, Houston.

"*KAVKA*/40": In my
memory, my father's Navy
picture resembles Kafka,
but I think even Kafka
wouldn't look like Kafka in
a U.S. Navy uniform. This
is from the early 1940s.

My father resembles Kafka
more in this undated photo,
probably from the late 1930s
or early 1940s, when he was
in his early twenties.

"HOLOCAUST GIRLS/CLOSET":
Rosi and I (*right*) before we moved
to the new house with walk-in closets
that made perfect hideouts from the
Nazis. My Barbie is emerging from
a Hanukah candy container, which
may have been used to store her
clothes. It is October 1961. When I
returned to visit the house more than
thirty years later, the striped curtains
were still there.

"The Language of *Heimatlos*": Herschel went dancing at El Dorado at 4 boulevard Strausbourg in Paris. In 1997 it was still a dance club.

Herschel bought a 6.35 mm revolver for 210 francs and a box of twenty-five bullets for 35 francs at À La Fine Lame, 61 rue du Faubourg St.-Martin. This is the site in 1997.

"Vacation at Club Dead": Children of the refugee camp in San Salvador, 1984.

"The Children of Theresienstadt": This is a little building in Theresienstadt – a small change booth and maybe a ticket entrance. I was struck by the signs for commercial aspects of the camp, now that it's a tourist spot – including restaurant and glass (glassware for sale? alcohol?).

Here are the "children of Theresienstadt," in (mostly) matching T-shirts, at their fiftieth reunion at the concentration camp.

"Getting to Yiddish": This is the "original" S. L. Wisenberg, my grandfather Solomon Louis Wisenberg, before he left Kishinev, circa 1905–1910. He was probably named after another S.L.W., who was named after another. . . . My aunt Dorothy thinks that he looks prosperous for a prospective émigré. I wonder if he borrowed the props.

"MARGOT'S DIARY": This is the
Franks' house in Frankfurt, where
Anne spent her first few years.

An Italian POW shared a machine with her and left food for her. "My husband says compared to others mine was a sanatorium," she says.

She was lucky, she says. "When we arrived we were fortunate our lice did not have typhus."

She tells the young American Jews of her lucky life. Among the Czechoslovaks, she says, there were few heroes who hid Jews. But there weren't active anti-Semites. She has no harsh words for the Czechs and Slovaks.

What she is bitter about is how her ninety-five-year-old mother has fared in America. She, the daughter, has approached several Jewish organizations to interview her mother. Nobody will take her oral history, she says.

The interviewers, she says, are looking for survivors from Poland. They don't want to hear from Jews from Czechoslovakia who have nothing bad to say about their countrymen.

The Americans notice her grinning. Later they remark on it to each other.

The smiling woman speaks of her son. She and her husband brought him here to visit the camp in 1977. "He's always trying not to face anything disagreeable," she says.

§

More than a year later, one of the young Americans sits in a bookstore audience in the Midwest listening to a Hungarian-American Jew talk about her book about life before and after Auschwitz. The woman writer's lips are parted, you can see her teeth, her eyes are distant – she's grinning. The young American who was in Theresienstadt in 1992 recognizes the expression. She calls it the Auschwitz smile because she can think of nothing more horrible to call it. A smile to bridge then and now. Or to keep the past and present apart.

§

In the museum in Theresienstadt is a sign: "In 1942 the ashes of the deceased were deposited in wooden urns. Later, paper urns were used."

The director of the museum says that later ashes were also thrown into the river.

The director had been a sociology professor at Charles University in Prague. He was born in 1946, has a bushy black and white goatee and mustache, and a round face, glasses. He's bald. He's the first Jewish director of the museum. Both of his parents went through the camps, both lost their first spouses in the war.

The Americans eat lunch with him, then return. They go to see crematoria, which are like huge iron lungs with trays at the end. The trays were for moving bodies in; now they contain pieces of ash and bone. Could these little gray and white bits be fifty years old? Is it possible?

The tummler asks a caretaker. The tummler tries out most of his languages in order to ask, concludes that nothing has been changed since liberation. He collects some of the . . . crumbs to take home with him. The other Americans take pictures. On one tray is a little shrine of lighted candles. On another are cards and notes and banners from visitors: "We remember" in heavy block letters from a group from Cleveland, Ohio; a handwritten note saying, ". . . and will do everything in our power to make sure nobody forgets."

The tummler has brought a banner of his own. Outside the crematoria, he lays the banner down. He asks the men in T-shirts, the survivors, to join him in saying the Kaddish, the prayer for the dead. They do, awkwardly, reluctantly, politely, trying to please.

Are they still Jewish? Do they believe in prayers for the dead?

The doctor from Philadelphia is embarrassed.

It is spectacle, the Jews from America arriving with a flourish and decorations, reciting Kaddish in a concentration camp, among stone memorials with the names of countries from which the dead came.

Near them is a new memorial stone to commemorate the visit of Chaim Herzog, president of Israel, just eight months before. "My sorrow is continually before me," it says, in Hebrew, English, and Czech. It is his standard stone left in concentration and death camps he has visited. His calling card.

§

It is easy to be ironic. To be distant. Because Theresienstadt – Terezín – is a museum, and old buildings and newly painted signs. A restaurant, a change booth. You can buy ice cream at Theresienstadt. At the exhibits there are few people. A video monitor beams out to a crowd or to emptiness. A man on the video speaks. He says: Every day here was like a year. A man on the video says: There was a plan to exchange children for Allied dollars but it fell through. And:

There was a coffeehouse in the camp where prisoners imitated Benny Goodman, providing "two hours of bliss."

In the museum is a sign that tells of a corner of life in Nazi-occupied Czechoslovakia in 1942: "Buying a canary, the customer had to sign a declaration that no Jews lived in the household." For Jews were not allowed the privilege of owning pets, or the pleasure of hearing by chance the brightness of a neighbor's songbird.

The Americans born after the war struggle to grasp it – the Holocaust – hoping that one, two, three different forms of media will cut through to the heart and brain. Why are the Americans there, after all, if *not* to say Kaddish? What are they trying to grasp? The Holocaust is the real thing. It's important to study it.

§

Theresienstadt was originally a garrison town built in the 1780s as fortification against Prussian attack. Soon it became a prison for military and political prisoners of the Austro-Hungarian Empire. One of its more famous was Gavrilo Princip, assassin of Austrian Crown Prince Franz Ferdinand. Princip lived in solitary.

There's something pretty about the reddish stucco walls mottled by time. And faded bricks in shades of rust. (Though "Arbeit Macht Frei" has been repainted sharply, neatly, in black over an archway.) It is still quiet enough, untouristed enough (though 150,000 people passed through the year before, barely more than during the war) that a person could lose herself in the place. Could walk away from her group of friends and stand in a barracks and wait for ghosts. There aren't any left. It is hard to people the empty rooms, to fill them with pained bodies. It is quiet. The quiet brick gives off a kind of beauty of poverty, of faded Third World buildings.

There must be some evil in that.

§

After the car trip to Theresienstadt, some of the young Americans feel bound together for life. A new subset of friends: People you went to Theresienstadt with; the people who saw the former prisoners in white T-shirts and pieces of people who died. And sunlight coming through windows onto slabs where gold teeth were removed. And memorial stones standing in for gravestones, over a former mass grave. And the big sign in Czech, English, and German, with a yellow

Star of David and schematic drawing of an archway, announcing, "Muzeum Ghetta. Daily opened."

Sometimes, sitting alone in Chicago, Austin, Philadelphia, Columbus, Berkeley, the Americans find it hard to believe – the banners, the Kaddish, the T-shirts – but after all, they have the photographs.

AFTERWARDS

My father's friend Harold Raizes told my father about living wills. Harold brought my father one and my father signed it and Harold signed his and they put them away. I don't know where. Took them to safe deposit boxes, most likely. Or to Melvin Cohn, the lawyer. (There's an old story my father used to tell. When he and my mother were in their early years of marriage, my father had Melvin draw up their wills. My father signed his and sent it back. My mother wouldn't sign it – it gave her the creeps, probably the same way she shivers whenever anyone mentions cats. She scrunches up her eyes and shoulders and her body shakes a little. So my mother's will sat and sat, unsigned and unsent. Finally my father called Melvin and asked him to call my mother and tell her there'd be an extra charge if she didn't send it back right away. So Melvin called my mother. And she complied. I don't know when my father let my mother in on the secret but he used to tell the story in front of her and she'd look embarrassed, caught, and laugh.)

When my sister and I used to fight, and I mean when we were already both out of college, my father would say, "Some day when we're gone, you're going to be all that's left," and we would say, "That's silly." Meaning: It's not that serious. We won't fight over your will. Our disagreements don't go that deep. The three of us – my mother, sister and I – thought he was getting morbid, melodramatic.

§

Richard Nixon had also signed a living will. After his death, I heard on the radio that one of five Americans have signed such documents. The reporter threw the fact of that in our faces, our ears rather, with the testimony of a woman – I almost said widow – whose husband was seriously injured in an accident and lay in a nursing home, no longer a thinking person. That man had not made a living will. The woman told NPR something along these lines: "He didn't want to be kept alive if anything like this happened. He said if I let him live that way, he'd haunt me every day of his life. And he has."

That day I heard the broadcast cycle twice, caught the woman's underlying, unsaid protest: It was a Friday night, we were going to dinner with our family. It was an ordinary treat in an ordinary life. How could fate have crossed our path like that? Is it too much to ask in this world to go out to dinner in peace?

§

My father hated going shopping. He didn't like waiting for my mother when she was shopping, only partly because she comes from a long line of people who can't make up their minds. Large items, small – cars, suits – he bought what was there, as quickly as possible, and was done with it. On a Saturday one August he took my mother to the airport for a fifty-five-minute flight from Houston to Dallas, where she was going to visit her parents. (In their nineties, frail.) My father took my mother to the airport and said, "Are you really going to leave me all alone?"

Then he went to Walter Pye's, a local department store, where there was a big sale on men's clothing. The sale was ending that day, I believe.

§

We were sitting in the waiting room we'd taken over. It was maybe Monday or Tuesday, and a man from Walter Pye's came to see us. He couldn't have expected to be allowed to see my father, because at that point, though the family had the run of his room – we could go in there whenever we wanted – it was out of bounds for others. I think. All I remember is the man seemed, this is the best word for it, tetched. He was laughing nearly hysterically while he said, "You go to buy some clothes, and look what happens, look what happened to Avrohm Wisenberg."

I'm not capturing it. The man was nervous. I think he meant to say something about irony, that no activity is a safe one, that by now we're used to people being kidnapped in shopping malls and stabbed in parking lots, but felled by a heart attack while trying on clothes –. And he wanted to absolve Walter Pye's of any guilt. The clothes didn't kill my father, after all.

He wasn't dead yet. Though I think he died while he was trying on clothes and I wonder if in a few generations, when we're all gone and there are a couple of great-great-grandchildren interested in family history, one of them will say off-handedly to a friend: "Did you know my great-great-grandfather died while he was trying on clothes?"

So Walter Pye's was having a big sale, it was possibly the last day of it, a Saturday, a day when many doctors are not in their offices, and some of them were in a nearby dressing room. Just after the salesclerk noticed my father's feet under the door, two doctor-shoppers gave my father CPR. And an ambulance came and someone in the store knew our family and called one answering machine after the other until he located my sister's husband's sisters's husband, who had no idea what to say when asked about my father's medical history.

Which tells you as much as anything else what it's like to be Jewish in Houston, to have decades of roots in the place, and thus be part of a network of people who grew up together and do business together and shop together.

Phone calls were made, airplanes were taken, and my brother-in-law picked me up from the airport Sunday, where I flew in from Chicago. I didn't think to ask about the bloody shirt in the back of his van. I found out later that my father had been wearing it. My Uncle Charlie had volunteered, too, to pick me up – my widowed, childless great-uncle who was slowly dying of cancer and liked to make himself useful – but I preferred someone my own age to get me, a friend-relative, and I had that luxury of choosing who would greet me at the airport and take me to the hospital. Later, in the hospital, my uncle asked, "Why couldn't it have been me instead of Avrohm?" My uncle was about fifteen years older than my father, had become intimate with the idea of his own death.

§

My father's chest was rising rhythmically, the perfect kind of deep breathing you're supposed to do, only his was powered by a machine. You could go in there and talk to him and look at him – his eyes were open but not looking at anything. He wasn't there. He wasn't there but it took us all a few days to figure it out, days in which his eyes kept getting more and more clouded over until there was no way he could come back to life, ever, not with eyes leaving him like that. The young doctor who'd been my father's internist twitched his lips whenever he approached us gathered in the waiting room, seemed almost amused that we were talking about him – father, husband – as if he were still a person, because he, this doctor, already knew that my father was just a body, my father's life was over. The young doctor told us the number of days or hours there were left of possibility – after that, there was no way my father could revive. Harold Raizes came to the waiting room, and by then we knew about the living will, and then others of my father's friends came, and my uncle from Dallas who showed us how to open small Perrier bottles using only a nickel and thumb pressure, and my aunt and uncle from Oklahoma, and aunt and uncle from Houston and my father's friend Harold Turboff who came through with his son who was in the same hospital recuperating from a skiing accident. Harold Turboff was the father of someone who would walk out of the hospital, however unsteadily.

§

There was an honor guard waiting outside Nixon's hospital room, waiting for the signal that he had died. Jews are not supposed to make preparations for a funeral while the person is still alive. The point is, I guess, to concentrate on the life still within the person, to not think ahead and miss the last moments. But what happens when you have a living will and it says no extraordinary measures, and in other words it means, *If I am shopping in Walter Pye's, and I have an aneurysm that bursts (because that seems to have been what happened, not a heart attack), and I fall and I'm seemingly revived but my brain is gone because it was deprived of oxygen, and I'm lying in a bed and slowly losing my face, my self, then disconnect me from the machines, stop the breaths that electricity is making me take, making it look like I'm taking, in short, pull the plug. Because I've already been dead for hours now. Days.*

When it was clear my father was not going to turn back into himself, the rabbi, my uncle, the doctor, and I think a nurse went into the hospital room. I went in too. The only member of the immediate family. My uncle is married to my father's younger sister. My sister and mother stayed in the waiting room. My uncle put his hands on my shoulders. The rabbi read the Twenty-third Psalm. My father, like a lot of other men who were boys in the 1930s, used to know an old old parody of it: "The Ford is my auto. I shall not want another. . . ." I read from Ecclesiastes because I thought that summed it up much better: The race is not to the swift. Vanity vanity, all is vanity.

And then he died. Officially. He was a few weeks shy of seventy-one.

A year later I was talking to someone who moved out of state so she could be with her ailing parents. She told me about the night her father died. She heard him, heard what she realized later was the death rattle, and stayed in her room. She didn't want to intrude upon his death. When she said that, I told her about my father's death and said I that later I felt voyeuristic about it, that I shouldn't have been there, I had no right to watch. It was private. We were killing him and then decided to watch. How obscene.

Another year passed during which I felt queasy still when I thought of it, standing there, and why was my uncle, his brother-in-law there, too? And didn't the rabbi feel ridiculous? Say a prayer, pull the plug. The prayer to say before pulling the plug. In the appendix of the all-purpose prayer book. For the '90s. The only thing that might make sense is that somewhere in the back of his mind my father might have known that this was going to happen as he died, and so it was befitting, it was necessary. He expected it. He lived his life with the unstated assumption that the Twenty-third Psalm would be said as he died and that in some way animated and informed a small small portion of his life.

A Jewish guidebook on death that I've just bought tells me, "It is a matter of greatest respect to watch over a person as he passes from this world on to the next." I suppose it is an honor to be there while the soul leaves the body, a comfort to the dying the stay with him till the end. But to witness the moment when the doctor cuts off the breath?

§

In Philip Roth's memoir, *Patrimony*, he tells about his father's brain tumor, describes how his eighty-six-year-old father asks the surgeons for one more year, then three and four, and Roth imagines the father finally demanding "only what I deserve – another eighty-six years!"

(As impossible as the solution to the dilemma in a joke I used to tell that my father took as his own: A shopkeeper comes home from his store during lunch and sees his head clerk on the couch with the shopkeeper's wife. He runs to the rabbi for advice. "He's my best clerk," the man tells the rabbi, "I can't fire him. She's an excellent wife," he tells the rabbi, "I can't divorce her." The rabbi tells him to return in a week. The man does, absolutely beaming. "What," asks the rabbi, "you fired the clerk?" "No." "You divorced your wife?" "No. I sold the couch!")

§

It was the way my father wanted it. That is true. That's why he signed the document that Harold Raizes brought him, that's why Nixon signed his. (For Nixon, too, as well, pride, I imagine, played a role: He didn't want to go down in history as the president who lingered, reduced to unconscious processes. And for the same reason, Reagan has officially absented himself from the scene after sending his hand-written letter about Alzheimer's to the press. He wants control of his last image.) But we know, all of us, it wasn't the way they wanted it. The way they wanted it was to stay another seventy-, eighty-odd years. And to stay the same.

At my father's funeral the rabbi recited the ancient words: "A man's time is three score and ten. . . ."

I counted up. Seventy? Only seventy? He WAS seventy. How could they say seventy? How could they say eighty, even, or ninety?

In a little pamphlet the rabbi gave us there's a story, taken from the Buddhists, about a woman who grieved and grieved because her son died, and she would not bury him. A wise man told her to go from house to house and bring back a mustard seed from a family that had not known sorrow.

And of course she went from house to house around the world and found everyone had been touched by sorrow and then she returned home. And buried her son.

§

In Jewish tradition, you keep a pitcher or bowl of water outside your door just after the funeral, so that people coming from the cemetery can wash their hands, can purify themselves after contact with the death. *Tumah*, the uncleanliness is called. My mother, my sister, and I decided not to set out the pitcher of water. "Old-fashioned," my mother said. But the older traditionalists, remnants of a dying gener-ation, reproached us as they entered our house. Explained clean and unclean to us, as if we hadn't known. They could not imagine that we could know tradition and not carry it out. There was of course a rea-son. At heart, we could not accept that my father was unclean, sepa-rate from us. And that someday in turn we will be separate, different, from what we are now.

There's another tradition, of serving boiled eggs after the funeral, a symbol for continuing life. We did that. That was easy.

While my father was still on machines, the doctor with the twitchy lips said, "He's healthy." Meaning, If not for the aneurysm, he'd have been in fine shape. His heart was beating soundly. We said, "This is the first time a doctor said he was healthy." He had a lot of health problems, small and medium. Everyone in the family did. He would say of my grandmother, "She's enjoying poor health." He would say, "Do you know what the hypochondriac's gravestone said – 'I told you I was sick.'" When we went to the cemetery for a funeral (everyone we knew was buried in that cemetery, it seemed, from my sister's friend who died of Hodgkin's just after college, to the grandfather I'm named after) my father would walk on our plot and say, "I'm checking out our property." My mother would cringe: morbid.

§

Ashkenazi Jews name their babies after the dead. I was proud to be named for my father's father, who died a year before I was born. Similar Hebrew names (his Shalom Layb became my Shulamit Leah), American names (Solomon Louis, Sandra Leah), same last name. I was proud when I went to services on the anniversary of his death and stood on the pulpit in the chapel while the rabbi praised my grandfather and our whole family. Then we'd sponsor the corned-beef-and-rye dinner afterwards. My father would always point out that the Kaddish, the mourner's prayer, does not have the word "death" in it.

Jewish tradition holds that for eleven months after the death of a member of your immediate family, you go to synagogue every morning and evening to say Kaddish. I've read that the reason, if it can be called that, is this: The worst possible person, the most evil, is condemned to be punished by God for at least twelve months after his death. We assume that our loved ones were better than that, so we pray for eleven months.

I didn't say the prayer twice a day. I thought about going to my neighborhood synagogue in Chicago for morning and late afternoon services. But I hardly know anyone at that synagogue; I am not part of that community, and none of them knew my father, who died eight hundred miles away in Texas.

I observe the anniversary of my father's death, but that's all. And I dream about him. At first the dreams were obviously about my coming to terms with his death. In them, he was slowly detaching himself from this world. Now he's just there, not a major character, not solely in the background, either – mostly a presence. He's alive, but there's something of the past about him, his suits are old, he often looks off in the distance. Last night I dreamed that my mother was divorcing him. We were at a huge gathering; my mother was animated, my father quiet, rejected, talking softly with a couple of friends. In real life, my mother is moving to a condo in a few weeks; she sold the family house a couple of months ago, after spending weeks painfully going through drawers and closets she hadn't been able to face before.

Last month, when I saw her at Thanksgiving in Dallas, along with dozens of other relatives from her side of the family, I noticed that she had moved her engagement ring to her right hand, no longer wore her wedding ring. That weekend was alive with children; one of them was a toddler named Adam, my cousin's son, named after my father.

§

I am growing used to having a dead father. My father has become someone to recall, to quote almost casually. My mother and sister and I have our little rituals: On the anniversary of my father's death I call my mother; on Father's Day she calls me and my sister; on my father's birthday my sister and her children buy lottery tickets, which my father talked about more often than bought. I find it strange that people assume that I have parents, plural, and ask me, for example, if they still live in Texas.

My father died in August 1991. How could that be truer? I can't quite believe he's underneath the ground, though I saw the casket lowered there, right in front of me, on our property. When I'm in airports, there's always an older man in a suit who looks, for a second, like my father. When the phone rings, for a moment, I think he might be on the other end. I'm reading *The Jewish Way in Death and Mourning*, by Maurice Lamm, and regretting that we didn't light candles around the deathbed, we didn't tear our clothes, that I didn't follow the other rules and customs of an *onen*, a mourner. A few days after my father died I returned to Chicago (flying at the "bereavement rate" provided by the airlines, as long as you can provide an obituary as proof) and to my life: I worked, I listened to music, I went to a birthday party.

Regret doesn't come from feeling I'm a bad Jew, but from feeling that I missed performing the traditional rituals that emphasize the significance of the death: Stop in your tracks. Your life is no longer the same. Mourn deeply for seven days. Avoid pleasure for thirty days. Recite the Kaddish for eleven months.

§

I have been thinking about the purpose of saying Kaddish; I can't bring the time back, can't decide, now, to recite it twice a day, just as we can't bring back the dead. The purpose of the eleven months of mourning, I've decided, isn't so much to pray for the souls under divine judgment or to get us out of the house and associating with other mourners (though that's what my father always said, another example of the practicality of the religion, he would offer, as if selling something) and it isn't even so much to comfort us with the thought that we'll be remembered just as we remember others – well of course it's all that, but there's more. With every breath of the Kaddish prayer that becomes more familiar than names of streets or phone numbers, that becomes a chorus, a chant, a mantra – a groove of belief is etched onto our brains, in order to make the words stay, stick with us, to force us to finally understand: he's gone he's gone he's gone.

GETTING TO YIDDISH

My grandfather was trained as a tailor. He left the Old Country in his teens, leaving a town called Kishinev, as in the Yiddish expression, All the way out in Kishinev, like we say or used to say, All the way to Timbuktu, except Kishinev was known as a place where *people* lived, *people* meaning *Jewish* people. The place is still on the map, it hasn't moved, as borders have risen and fallen, so that Kishinev has been a city in Romania, or Rumania, or the capital of Moldavia, USSR, and now, Moldova, NIS – Newly Independent States. In 1903 there was a bloody pogrom there, the violence of which shocked the world, the Jewish world as well as the non-Jewish, was protested by Theodore Roosevelt and Leo Tolstoy. My sister says my aunt says my grandfather remembered the pogrom. We know for sure that he left, leaving behind his sister, mother, and maybe a brother, he came to New York alone, early 1900s, alone but in the middle of a sweep of immigrants from Eastern Europe, welcomed by Lady Liberty. That poem, "Give me your tired, your poor, / Your huddled masses yearning to breathe free," was written by a Jew. Who had not ever been among those huddled masses; her people came from Spain and Germany, her native language was English. My grandfather as a teenager arrived by boat via Hamburg, knowing Yiddish, Hebrew, and probably Russian, German, Romanian, or Moldavian. Fat German law books came with him or after him. They rest in my mother's condo, leather-clad and old. My grandfather stayed with People. *Landslayt*, we imagine – Jewish people from his home region.

There are two New York stories about him. One is that he wore a beautiful black suit from home, which he had carefully and painfully sewn himself, and that the other fellows in America made fun of it, the old-fashioned cut, the unknowing greenhornness of it. But I may have made that story up. I used it in a short story I wrote in grad school. In my story, the suit is made of gabardine, the relatives give him a hand-me-down suit that is more up-to-date, they give him a place to sleep on their dovecote, a word he tasted and wondered over and loved. This next story is true, meaning that it is a true family story, told by my father. In this story, my grandfather comes to New York, stays with the landslayt, becomes frustrated because he's not learning English, so leaves for Macon, Georgia. (Where else?) It is true he wound up in Macon. It may be true that he went South to find English. Perhaps the Lower East Side was too small and crowded, too much like home.

In Macon he worked his way through the Hall School, a prep school for young Southern gentleman, a place where boys did not merely pass through to "'get a diploma,' as most of our schools are throughout the State, but an institution of thorough scholarship, fellowship, friendship, and good citizenship." S. L. Wisenberg, president of the senior class of 1914, wrote that in a school pamphlet. Another school document shows that he taught Greek and German. My father used to say that he was really teaching Hebrew and Yiddish.

My grandfather was trained as a Southern gentleman. He passed the Georgia bar exam in the days when that was enough to make you a lawyer. He supported a district attorney candidate who was going to appoint him assistant if he won. The man lost.

My grandfather met my grandmother at a regional Zionist conference. She was from Pusvatin, in Kovno-gubernia, and more recently, Selma. The couple ran a dry goods store in Laurel, Mississippi, where her family had moved. His mother came to visit from Kishinev. She spoke no English, kept a vehement kosher, had conversations with a Gentile neighbor in who-knows-what language, ate lemon drops, then returned to Moldavia/Moldova to die.

During the Depression, the family moved to Houston. My grandfather started a new business, the kind of business you can start if you have nothing with which to buy something to sell. He sold insurance – safety, guarantees, promises to help people, Jews, out in time of need. He had diabetes, which he didn't monitor, he was not in good health. My father returned from the War and was trained to run the family business. My grandfather kept kosher, and so instead of nonkosher meat he'd order eggs scrambled in butter when he went to lunch every day at One's a Meal. He died of a heart attack at sixty, a year or two before I was born.

My grandfather was trained as a tailor. My father was trained in economics and dreamed of law school and becoming a Supreme Court justice, like Louis Brandeis. My aunts on both sides went to college. My mother's college education at the University of Texas was doled out a year at a time, by her father. For both of my parents, Yiddish was the secret language of the grown-ups, which they spoke when the children were around. My mother minored in Spanish. Both of my parents took elocution lessons. In high school my father won a citywide prize for debate.

My grandfather was trained as a tailor, my father was trained in economics and the family business, my mother took a degree in education. For my sister and me, Yiddish was the name of a few words that peppered the language, especially at family gatherings. *Ponim* – face. *Potsh* – a slap (a threat). My father would say "Zets zik avek dortn," just for the sound of it, as well as "Esn, fresn in the delicatessen" the same way he'd chant, "I must go where the wild goose goes, wild goose, brother goose, which is best, a wandering goose or a goose at rest?" In Houston public schools starting in third grade, my sister and I learned Spanish, we learned Hebrew in the late afternoons at Hebrew school, in preparation for our bat mitzvahs. At Hebrew school, young Israeli women with no idea of pedagogy taught us grammar and vocabulary from flimsy textbooks. We didn't ask what for, or why not Yiddish. We assumed we were learning Hebrew so we could read the prayer book and holy books, so we could speak when we visited Israel, but most of all because we were Jews, and that's what Jews knew. I had no idea then that Yiddish had vied with Hebrew to be designated the national language of Israel. In high school I learned French because I loved its sophistication. In college I studied in Paris. Throughout college I had little interest in being a practicing, God-fearing Jew. I wrestled with myself and the religion and customs. In graduate school I lived in a small town and became a pacifist and went to Quaker meeting and organized small Shabbat dinners. I moved to Miami and wrote for a newspaper. I wrote about retired socialist Jews on Miami Beach and with them listened to a speech by Paul (Peysekh) Novick, the nonagenarian editor of the *Morning Freiheit*. He spoke in Yiddish. The only parts I understood were "Mondale" and his fervor.

My mother's grandfather was a Jewish émigré blacksmith in Dallas. The profession of my father's grandfather in Kishinev is lost to history. My grandfather was trained as a tailor, my father was trained in business, my mother was trained in education, I was trained as a writer. My father taught me how to thread a needle. We call this progress, the American dream, the way my grandfather eventually bought a house of his own, and a car, and helped start a synagogue and printed out business cards and calendars to give away to promote his insurance agency, and, everyone said, told jokes to lighten the gloom set by my grandmother. He did this all in English, and after he died, the next-born grandson took his name, and then the next-born granddaughter was given a variation of his name, so that there are now two S. L. Wisenbergs; one was an assistant to Kenneth Starr, and the other is me.

It's been my belief for some time that part of the American trauma is our shared sacrifice of leaving behind. Language, family, community, land. Gone, gone gone.

In the early 1990s I began doing research on German and East European Jews, in particular and in general. I was interested in one woman in particular, Bertha Pappenheim, born in Vienna in 1859, famous on two fronts. She was a sort of Jane Addams of her time, but also she was the famous Anna O., the first case described in Freud and Breuer's *Studies on Hysteria*. Bertha was upper crust, a generation removed from the ghetto, a product of select Catholic schools for girls. She made lace, she spoke French and English, and for any number of reasons which could include her father's sickness and death, she became a hysteric and was cured or not. In the 1880s she moved with her mother to Frankfurt and joined her cousins in charity work. One day she was helping at a soup kitchen for Eastern European Jewish refugees. She started talking to a lonely little girl in line. They spoke in Yiddish, and Bertha found her people and her vocation. Orphan and destitute Jewish girls, they became the focus of her work. She spoke a fine German, to officialdom, but to her adopted "daughters" – charges from across Europe – she spoke Yiddish.

Yiddish – the magic tongue that connects, high to low, usually low to low. Yiddish is the *mameloshn*, the mother tongue, the language of the shtetl, the Jewish village, the language of the immigrants – to Frankfurt, Berlin, Paris, New York, Chicago, Montreal, Omaha, Galveston, Buenos Aires . . . Macon, Georgia. The language of speeches by Eugene Debs and Fiorello LaGuardia, and union meetings and newspapers, movies, avant-garde theater pieces, the talk of the home, the factory, the women – because only the men knew the formal language that God spoke, Hebrew. Yiddish was the old shoe, the jargon, the way you spoke to Jews from other provinces and lands, not the language of literature until Sholom Aleichem, a stockbroker from Kiev, used it to create the life of Tevye the Milkman.

The language that my grandfather left behind in Kishinev had no place, he thought, in the New World, America, where you could become a free citizen, a Jew could become a Supreme Court justice, a film star, a radio comedian, a merchant, a city official – and college was free or nearly so, and if you didn't like where you were living, you could pick up and move. Again and again.

The grandfathers of citizens of the U.S. spoke Spanish, Chinese, Polish, German, Japanese, Urdu, Italian, Swahili, Arabic, Hebrew, Algonkian, French, Tagalog, creoles of many sorts, and so on and so on. This is not news. It is also not news that we have been yearning for our elusive roots, as glowing as the *goldeneh medineh*, promised land, of America, yearning in the open since the 1960s. Because we're no longer afraid. Because our forebears sacrificed their old ways, we became secure enough, American enough, to long for a taste of the old ways.

To research Bertha I took German. At the first Goethe-Institut class, the other Jew in the room and I found each other immediately: During the break we agreed that the class reminded us of words from old war movies. In another class, we learned past tense, and it seemed natural, right, that you made a verb past tense by, in general, adding, ge. As in the Yiddish *gemakht, gegesn*. Sounded familiar, in my gut, my Yiddish soul.

I decided I would take Yiddish if I came across a class. I saw a course in a catalogue and signed up. First I met the teacher for a private session to learn a few basics. She taught me the letters to make up *oy*, the universal Jewish cry. She wrote a few words on the yellow legal pad we were using, including, by chance, Avroym.

My father's name was Avrohm. A Hebrew name, we always said, though that wasn't a name we'd come across in the books in the synagogue. A little twist and Avrohm becomes Avroym. A Yiddish name. My father had died four years before. I am taking Yiddish, I thought, as a memorial to him.

Every Monday I go to the class. It's in a synagogue in Rogers Park on Chicago's North Side. We sit in the small chapel. The teacher is *frum* – religious – she wears a wig and tells jokes, and has a Ph.D. There are a few other religious women, and at least one who is secular and who learned the language as a child in a Yidishe-shule in Chicago, culture and language classes set up by the socialist, nonreligious immigrants.

The class feels comfortable. I learn that ordinary things we said growing up, for example, *Gut Shabes* (Good Sabbath) *Gut yontev* (Good holiday) were Yiddish, but that my grandmother's English expression "Wear it in good health" was of Yiddish origin. I learn why my father's pronunciation of Hebrew was different from mine – He learned under the influence of Yiddish speakers, and I, under the guidance of impatient Israelis.

I can intellectualize, spiritualize the reasons for taking Yiddish in the third millennium: honoring our parents, honoring the Yiddish speakers who died during the war, which, among other things, was a war against Yiddish. But class is fun. It feels homey, *heymish*; going to class is the most consistent Jewish thing I do. You don't have to believe in God to study Yiddish, you have to believe in the Jewish people. Which may be idolatry to some. Every week, I go to the Orthodox synagogue and in the language of my ancestors discuss movies and plays and birthdays and sickness. We read in our text about Moyshe in New York writing to his relatives overseas. We learn dative and accusative. We talk about holidays. I am afraid of being found out, as a "modern woman," with a lover and no children, but I think I've already been found out and, I hope, accepted. In a Jewish world that is fragmented, where some of the Orthodox condemn the rest of us, where the very religious are the only ones who have embraced

Yiddish as a daily tongue, along with the black gabardine clothes of the ghetto and the *peyes* and beards and wigs – the ten or so of us, all women, sit in our jeans and long skirts around a table in a synagogue and laugh and laugh.

Some say Yiddish is dead, it hardly lives outside the classroom or archives. We don't know if we are part of a revival or are assisting at a slow death. We will never find out what our parents and grandparents were saying behind our backs. But I know what their words sounded like.

Monica and Hannah

1. Two Modern Girls

Two Jewish girls in their early twenties. Each from a large, famous city on the water, a city where Jews are prominent in the arts and entertainment. Each girl suffers a traumatic family event in childhood, has material comforts, an assimilated, modern life, attends exclusive schools. Both are especially close to their mothers. Neither is given a very rigorous Jewish education. They both love poetry – reading and writing it – they both think about becoming teachers someday. Both get in trouble with the government, as a result of their own daring actions.

The difference begins here: One is *zaftig* – which used to mean attractively juicy, and now means unattractively fat.

The other is thin.

Or: One comes of age in a time of regional political upheaval and violence. The other comes of age in a time of intermittent violence. The second one travels to the capital of the only superpower left on Earth and pleasures the leader of the Free World – but she is not a concubine. "The irony is that I had the first orgasm of the relationship," she says later.

The first one dies a virgin.

But we are getting ahead.

2. What Kind of Name Is Lewinsky, Anyway?

... the president asked, when she accused him of not knowing her name.

Her "riposte," writes biographer Andrew Morton, was "Jewish." Riposte?

They also shared dirty jokes, mostly Jewish. They went like this: Why do Jewish men like to see porno films backwards? Monica asked. So they can see the hooker give the money back. As for the President of the United States of America, he asked, "What do you get when you cross a Jewish American Princess with an Apple?" Answer: "A computer that won't go down on you."

An odd, odd choice considering whom he told it to. After all, according to *Salon,* though Monica was responsible for reviving the stereotype of the JAP, she also had a part in "the emancipation of her sisters from their perceived state as neurotic prudes."

Judging by the biography (as much as I could get myself to read), Monica has few positive associations with being Jewish, even if you do include the book *Oy Vey! The Things They Say: A Guide to Jewish Wit,* one of her many gifts to Clinton. Her childhood Conservative synagogue was too orthodox, Morton reports. She wanted a big bat mitzvah but her father offered only a backyard party. It's unclear from the biography whether Morton understands that a bat mitzvah is still at the core a religious occasion that takes place in a synagogue, no matter how outlandish and expensive the surrounding hoopla. Monica referred to it aptly as "a wedding for one." She ended up with a mere five hundred dollar party, with DJ and hotdog stand. I still can't figure out if she had the ceremony. We're also told she sang beautifully at her younger brother's bar mitzvah.

The bat mitzvah/party was a point of contention with her father. She was much closer to her mother, especially after her parents separated and divorced a year later.

Just about the only strength Monica drew from her religion was from the story of Hannah Senesh, a Jewish woman born in Hungary who became a martyr during World War II. Monica first learned about her from a Hollywood-style movie and wrote a school essay about her. They both had strong bonds with their mothers, Monica wrote. Though she herself was not as brave as Hannah. During the trying day when she was shut up (though not officially "detained"), lawyerless, in a hotel room with FBI agents and Starr deputies, thoughts of Hannah sustained her. Also that day, she was helped by reading the Ninety-first Psalm, which a Christian Science counselor had recommended to her. The counselor was recommended to her by her mother. Later she introduced Monica to a rabbi.

3. HANNAH

She was born in Budapest in 1921. She and her older brother were unaware they were Jewish until the brother went to school and was told. Their last name sounded Hungarian, because their father had changed it from the Jewish Schlesinger. The father, Bela Senesh, was a popular playwright and columnist, though his plays weren't performed at the National Theatre because he was Jewish. Ah well, he told his wife, his plays were "better suited" to the Comedy Theatre anyway. Other than that, they were not bothered much by anti-Semitism. Both Christian and Jewish writers and actors came to their villa to mingle and be witty. The parents were indulgent, trying to create the perfect childhoods for Hannah and George – storytelling sessions, trips to the zoo and lake – because they knew that Bela's time was short. He'd had rheumatic fever as a child and expected to die young. He did, at thirty-three, when Hannah was not quite six.

Hannah Senesh was brilliant and popular at school. From an early age she tutored other students. She wrote poetry early on – according to biographer Anthony Masters, as the only way to express her feelings – and hoped to become a writer, teacher, or organizer of a summer camp. At thirteen she started keeping a diary. She intended to write about "beautiful and serious things" and not stoop to focusing on boys and trivial matters, and chastised herself in print when she did. But, in addition to her thoughts on *War and Peace*, she did include descriptions of her ideal boy, of precocious marriage proposals, and of dance parties that lasted until 3 and 4 A.M. She even had a long blue dress, as Monica did.

Hannah attended an elite Protestant school where Jews had to pay three times as much as the regular tuition. If there were no discrimination, she'd have received a scholarship, according to her mother, who complained to the school. Eventually her tuition was lowered to the same price Catholics were charged. In 1937 she was elected an officer of her school's literary club, then was refused the title by other students because she was Jewish.

4. HOLY LAND I

After Hitler annexed Austria in 1938, neighboring Hungary passed laws discriminating against Jews. Hannah came to see Palestine as the place where Jews could become full citizens, and declared herself a Zionist. She learned Hebrew by correspondence course and applied for admission to a girls' agricultural school in Palestine. To prepare for the conditions, she spent a vacation gardening in the middle of the day, when the sun was the hottest. She left Budapest in September 1939, regretting only that she was leaving her mother alone. Her brother had already left, to study in France.

5. HOLY LAND II

Not much was made of Lewinsky's Jewishness – except by American Jews, anti-Semites, and the Arab media. And then there was her grandstanding ex-lawyer William Ginsburg, who, when still of counsel, told an Israeli newspaper such gems as, "Clinton is very positive toward Israel and the Jews, and Monica and I are Jews." When asked whether his client would seek asylum in Israel, he replied he didn't think so. He added that Monica would feel comfortable there.

American Jews discussed in print whether it was good for the Jews or bad for the Jews that Lewinsky was Jewish. There was Arab speculation that Mossad or the American-Jewish lobby was behind the conspiracy, aiming to keep Clinton preoccupied so he wouldn't push Benjamin Netanyahu on the peace process. Typical was Lebanese Premier Rafik al-Hariri, who was quoted by Reuters as saying, "The Zionist lobby is twisting the arm of the president of the greatest country in the world." Some Arab newspapers alleged that Lewinsky's actions were part of a plot to influence Clinton's Iraq policy.

6. LAUNDRY

Hannah grew up with a housemaid and was not used to doing chores. In Palestine there were no domestic servants. From her diary, February 9, 1942: "Today I washed 150 pairs of socks. I thought I'd go mad. No, that's not really true."

Palestine was filling up with Central European intellectuals who had come to work the land. At the agricultural school and later on a kibbutz near Caesaria, Hannah went to classes, washed laundry, scrubbed floors, sorted grapefruit, picked olives; served on guard duty, and worked in the dairy, bakery, garden, and chicken house. Occasionally she wondered what she was doing there and longed for satisfying work. She hoped she wasn't wasting her time. She wrote poetry in Hebrew, thought of becoming a writer – or a traveling poultry farming instructor. She had only one close friend, wrote in her diary "there are a few men who love me" – and yet she didn't love them. She wrote a play about a musician trying to figure out how much she owes herself and how much, the collective. She was lonely, but she concluded that she was happy she had immigrated, that she loved the land, that she would do it all over again. She became more committed to Zionism and socialism. She began to feel a sense of mission, a burning desire to stop the slaughter of Jews still in Europe.

7. THE MISSION

Senesh volunteered to parachute over the Balkans to collect intelligence for the British. Only two other women took the training. The young men and women learned judo, how to use knives and assemble and disassemble guns. The group was supposed to collect information on the enemy's positions, help downed Allied pilots, and organize Jewish resistance and rescue.

She and the others in the Hungarian Mission parachuted into Slovenia in March 1944. They spent about three months with Tito's partisans while waiting to cross the border. She grew restless, impatient to get to Hungary. In June she and another paratrooper left Yugoslavia. They were picked up almost immediately and taken to Budapest.

She was beaten and imprisoned. The Hungarian police brought her mother to the prison. Catherine Senesh found Hannah nearly unrecognizable – she had two black eyes, her face and neck were covered with welts and bruises, her thick hair was stringy and filthy. The police told Catherine: "Speak to her! Use your maternal influence and convince her she had better tell us everything, otherwise you'll never see each other again!"

Her mother decided that she would not try to influence her daughter, no matter what the cost. "If there was something Hannah did not want to reveal," Catherine Senesh wrote later, "she had good reason, and under no circumstances would I influence her otherwise."

Later her mother was sent to the same prison by the Gestapo.

8. LOST IN TRANSLATION

In a school essay, Monica wrote, "I wish that I had the inner conviction that Hannah Senesh had. I am not nearly half as brave as she was." Monica said Hannah's connection to her mother "could not be broken by anything and that is the same with me."

Morton writes: "The young Monica got the story a bit muddled after seeing the 1988 movie *Hanna's War*, and thought the Nazis had told Senesh that her mother would be killed unless she, Hannah, revealed details of the British spy network. . . . As a result of seeing the film she may have got parts of the story wrong – when Senesh was arrested, her mother was in fact living not in Hungary but in Palestine – but the love and loyalty illustrated in her version of it affected her deeply."

In fact, Morton got the story a bit muddled. When Hannah Senesh was brought to Budapest, her mother was still living there – she had been waiting five months for a visa to Palestine.

It's true that Lewinsky is no Senesh. But to her credit, when Starr's investigators offered her immunity – in exchange for taping conversations with Betty Currie, Vernon Jordan, maybe Clinton – she refused.

9. MENTAL HEALTH

I didn't read the book all the way through. This is why: For a week I'd been moodier and more anxious than usual, which is saying a lot, and assuaged my anxiety with generous amounts of coffee ice cream. The only possible explanation I could come up with for my black mood was this: I'd been reading *Monica's Story*. To read her biography is like taking a five-hour call from your most annoying friend when you were fourteen years old, the one with constant boy problems. The book is full of obsession with weight, hysterical middle-of-the night phone calls, hysterical waiting for middle-of-the-night phone calls, canceled plane reservations, silly flirtations, dangerous liaisons – desperations familiar from high school: He noticed her, he didn't notice her, she was cool toward him and that made him more interested, he didn't call, she wrote a letter and discussed it for hours with Linda Tripp. It's all so familiar, females at our worst. In junior high my friends and I would make little notebooks for ourselves, filled with beauty and diet and exercise and fashion tips from our monthly bibles – *Teen, Seventeen, Ingenue*. Another bible of that time, a sort of alchemist's book for preteens and teens, was *How to Get a Teen-Age Boy and What to Do with Him When You Get Him* by Ellen Peck. Judging by the jacket photo and bio, Peck was a hip-looking junior high school teacher complete with a Mary Travers un-hairdo and the pale frosty lips we all had in that era.

"Let's review some important principles," Peck writes. "First the best way to a boy is still through his crowd. . . . But if the guy doesn't have a crowd, approach solo. . . . Remember to be consistently friendly and outgoing. . . . Remember the idea is that you make the first move." Which is exactly how Lewinsky proceeded.

Peck also provides info on "When it all ends, what do you do?" Things to do: "One. Wait twenty-four hours before you do ANYTHING. . . . Two. Repeat this procedure for another twenty-four hours, meanwhile telling yourself this: 'I can eventually get him back.'" She also recommends spending money, appearing in public with other boys, even causally, and getting the word out that you want to date again. Lewinsky did try to get him back, but she wasn't so good at waiting.

After reading about her ordeal in the hotel room I put Lewinsky's book down. Why finish *Monica's Story*? I asked myself, I know what happens. I couldn't resist jumping to the conclusion of the book, where I learned that Monica is angered by the president's actions, loathes Linda Tripp, feels guilt and shame. She is "feisty" and "principled" and "indomitable" and talks about grad school, attaching herself to a worthwhile cause. She wants the episode behind her, wants to get married, be a wife and mother.

10. OUR NATIONAL OBSESSION

Look in the index, under "Lewinsky, Monica – weight" and you'll find nine citations, just one less than those under "immunity deal." And the indexer missed out on some of the mentions.

Weight becomes an issue early on in the book, on the third page of the foreword, when Morton describes meeting with Monica while she flips through family albums. She keeps mentioning how fat she looked in that picture, how she'd lost weight in that one. Morton ascribes her avoirdupois to low self-esteem, unhappiness with her parents' divorce. Like most biographies of the merely famous, this one discloses all the mundane aspects of a very ordinary childhood. Here, at least, a theme definitely emerges: At age nine, Lewinsky was called "Big Mac" because of her chubbiness. Summer before eighth grade, she was excited to be allowed to go to "fat camp" where she lost weight, and so the year started well. But the weight loss was short-lived. In high school she gained fifty pounds in less than a year. After she was banished from the White House for "overfamiliarity," she spent the weekend crying, eating pizzas and sweets.

One of the early times that Clinton noticed Lewinsky, she was flattered by his attention, but worried she might look fat "and therefore tried to suck in her stomach as she chatted to him. She also thanked her lucky stars that she was wearing black, a slimming color." The first time she unbuttoned his shirt, – in the presidential bathroom – he sucked in his gut. She thought it so endearing. "I said, 'Oh, you don't have to do that – I like your tummy.'" In one of their close confidential talks, he confessed details about his life as a fat boy. The best compliment, the savvy Clinton knew, was to comment on her weight loss. You're looking skinny, he said. You look good, he said. Once after they passed in the hallway, he called her to say she'd lost weight. When Lewinsky and Linda Tripp met in the Pentagon, at first they talked about dieting. Monica encouraged Tripp to lose sixty pounds on Weight Watchers. Of course, conspiring Democrats were behind Tripp's issues with food: "She told Monica that she had become a compulsive eater on the return flight from [Vince] Foster's funeral in Arkansas on board Air Force One."

While some affairs take their character from the wanton consumption of martinis or marijuana or champagne, this one confined itself to a more ordinary elixir. In order to disguise the true nature of their relationship, Lewinsky would leave the Oval Office with a Diet Coke in hand. "It looked a little more friendly and less sexual," she explained.

Who says that Clinton was unrestrained in his passions? After all, he refrained from imbibing the Real Thing.

11. WEIGHT AS FATE?

When the wife of on-again-off-again lover Andy Bleiler found out about their affair, Lewinsky brought out the fat card: she'd only slept with him because she was insecure about her weight.

In November 1997 Lewinsky planned to take the fateful blue Gap dress with her on a Thanksgiving trip in San Francisco. Tripp knew the dress had important evidence on it, and tried to convince her good friend to save it in a plastic bag, "for her own protection." When that didn't make much of an impression, she tried again, telling Monica she looked fat in the dress.

That did the trick. She wore something else, and put the dress back in her closet instead of taking it to the dry cleaner's.

Hannah's diary, July 22, 1937. "I'm as healthy as a horse. But they are forever trying to put me on a fattening diet."

In photographs, she is attractive enough – and thin – but easier to describe by what she is not: neither delicately featured nor classically beautiful. In any case, her looks did not seem to preoccupy her or her swains. She seemed to be satisfied with her reflection in the mirror. Do we ascribe Monica's and Hannah's self-images to culture or personality?

Is it personal or political? Psychological or social?

12. Man as Fate

When she was seven, Monica wanted to grow up to be president of the United States. She thought later of becoming a teacher. She loved poetry. In college she thought of getting a Ph.D. in forensic psychology and jurisprudence. But, damn those men, she was so upset about Bleiler that she did poorly on the GRE. One of the reasons that moving to Washington DC appealed to her was that Bleiler would be far, far away. Men were never far from her mind. During the many hours she was kept mostly in a hotel room by FBI agents, threatened with jail time, she said to Starr deputy Mike Emmick, "If I go to jail for twenty-seven years who is ever going to marry me? How will I be able to have children?"

13. Prison and Palestine

In jail Hannah Senesh acted the way you would want to have acted if you were ever imprisoned. She was warm, giving, intellectually alive. She taught her mother and other prisoners to speak Hebrew. She took a young girl under her wing. She argued about Palestine with her jailers. She stacked a chair and table on top of her bed and climbed up in order to see outside. She made paper dolls to cheer up other prisoners. She made her mother an anniversary present of handmade flowers of straw and paper.

The Soviets were bombarding the city. She told her guards that they'd have to answer to the Allies at the end of the war. Still she was tried for treason. Found guilty by a Hungarian military court. Would not ask for clemency. Was executed, by firing squad, on November 7, 1944. She refused a blindfold.

Her body was buried in the martyrs' section of the Jewish cemetery in Budapest, and a few years after Israel became a state, her remains were moved there and given a soldier's burial.

Editor and professor Marie Syrkin took the first ship from New York to Palestine after the war, fall 1945, to interview Holocaust survivors and resistance fighters. "Hanna Senesh has become a national heroine of Palestine and hers was the name which I heard most frequently upon my arrival," she wrote in the book *Blessed Is the Match: The Story of Jewish Resistance*, published in 1947. "Every Jew in Palestine," she wrote, "can recite the four simple lines of the poem Hanna wrote shortly before she was executed."

This is the poem, translated from the Hebrew by Syrkin:

Blessed is the match that is consumed in kindling flame.
Blessed is the flame that burns in the secret fastness of the heart.
Blessed is the heart with strength to stop its beating for honor's sake.
Blessed is the match that is consumed in kindling flame.

It has become part of a number of modern Haggadahs, the book used on Passover, which is constantly being updated and amended by feminists, vegetarians, parents, and religious leaders. The American poet Ruth Whitman translated Hannah's poem thirty years later ("Blessed is the match that burns and kindles fire") so that there is less of the martyr in it; it's less passive, more active. But the idea is the same.

Abba Eban wrote in 1971 that in Israel a ship, a forest, two farming settlements, and thirty-two streets had been named after Senesh. According to historian Livia Rothkirchen, there is also a species of flower.

Who will be the more well-known name of the twentieth century – the universally recognized Lewinsky, with her indelible smile and sought-after lipstick, or Senesh, who is probably unknown in most countries except Israel? These two young Jewish women, half a century apart, are as good examples as any of paths that privileged young Jewish women in the developed world can take, have open to them, make open to themselves.

Is that a fair statement? Is it fair to lump them together?

14. NATURE/NURTURE

They aren't the same. Times aren't the same. Losing a father to divorce is not the same as losing him to death. Budapest in the 1920s and '30s is not L.A. or Beverly Hills in the 1970s and '80s. A Monica Lewinsky born in 1921 in Budapest would not necessarily have immigrated to Palestine. But even before 1938 she probably wouldn't have been an intern in the unstable, ever-increasingly anti-Semitic government. A Hannah Senesh raised in Beverly Hills might have spent more and more time worrying about her body and boys and frivolities. But she probably would not have displayed her thong underwear to the president.

15. SPIN

Hannah is a hero, though she should not be romanticized, Syrkin was cautioning already in 1947. Years later, Abba Eban echoed her words that Senesh is not Joan of Arc.

Anthony Masters is the most cynical of her biographers, calling the whole plan to parachute young Palestinians into Central Europe "a suicide mission." Furthermore, he adds, "Quite what Hannah thought she was going to do once she had crossed the border was difficult to imagine; certainly she gave it little thought."

Her heroism was important for new state of Israel, he claims, because it helped "create nationalism."

16. THE MAKING OF AMERICANS

Lenny Bruce had a famous routine called Jewish and goyish. Chocolate is Jewish, fudge is goyish. Fruit salad is Jewish, lime Jell-O is goyish. All New Yorkers are Jewish. "Negroes are all Jews. Italians are all Jews. Irishmen who have rejected their religion are Jews. Mouths are very Jewish. And bosoms. Baton-twirling is very goyish." And so on.

In the first part of the twentieth century, immigrant Jews became American. In the second half, bagels and Yiddish became American, and more to the point, the Holocaust became American. Anne Frank seems American, part of the curriculum, part of Broadway. The Holocaust TV series was American. So was the list of Oskar Schindler, and so is the Holocaust museum in D.C.

Sigmund Freud has become American. So have ethnic Albanians and Nelson Mandela. Not to mention scones, pasta, and Zen Buddhism.

Hannah Senesh, born in Budapest, left her home because her country did not allow her to assimilate. She immigrated to Palestine and after she died, she became American.

§

When I finally went back to finish the last chapters of Lewinsky's biography, I found another young Jewish woman. After Monica and her mother had been subpoenaed, they became afraid that their conversations were being bugged. They were scared to death. "This was not how we should be living in America in this century," Lewinsky said later. "It reminded me of *The Diary of Anne Frank*. We were living in constant fear."

Margot's Diary

Photos: Anne, 1941; Margot, 1941:
They both part their hair on the left side, wear a watch on the same wrist, have the same eyebrows, same open-mouthed smile. Their noses and eyes are different, the shape of their faces, the cut of their hair, the fall of it. Books are open in front of each of them. One photo we glance past. Because she is unknown. We don't care what she looks like – she's vaguely familiar. Not the real one. She is the sister of. The shadow. The first child who made way for the second, the important one. Who is more alive. Whose photo is crisp in contrasts, not blurry.

The Diaries:
Margot kept one, you know. She was the daughter known to be smart, studious, reflective. Hers was lost. Among the many items lost in the war, among millions. Perhaps her diary was darker – she was older, quieter, frailer. More naturally introspective. Perhaps she did not write that she believed that people were good at heart. (Which is something Anne believed only some of the time, anyway.) Perhaps Margot did not rejoice in nature. Perhaps she wrote: "There must be something wrong with us or else they would not be after us. We are cooped up here like mice. Anne is the only one who seems not to know we are doomed but she may be the bravest of all. We learn our French for what. In order to learn our French. We will be so warped upon our exit here that if we ever do escape, if there ever is freedom, we will not be able to live among the others. We shall be marked more than by the outline of the yellow badges."

Why We Like Them:
They were suburban and then urban. They had bicycles and birthday parties. We know how to put both of those things together. Or whom to call to arrange them. The girls were just like us – the thrill of the avalanche missed.

Not that we would ever sacrifice someone else –

IN THE ANNE FRANK *HUIS*, AMSTERDAM:
Which was not a house, but an apartment over the office where her father had been in business selling pectin for making jellies, and spices for making sausages. In July 1992 a young girl on a tour smiles in recognition of Anne's familiar face in a photo. On the wall are French vocabulary words Anne copied out:

la poudre à canon
le voleur
la maison de commerce
le conseil
de retour
le gluie (het glure)
le musée
la cause
le bouquet
l'éducation
envie
après-demain
avant-hier
le sang

[gunpowder
thief
business-firm?
advice
returning back
glue?
museum
cause
bouquet
education
desire
the day after tomorrow
the day before yesterday
blood]

Five thousand visitors a year stream into the old narrow house. Often, there are lines.

IN FRANKFURT:

There's a plaque on the door of the duplex that was the first Anne
Frank house, which the family left the year of Hitler's election. They
went west, to Aachen, then Amsterdam, for safety. Someone lives in
the house still; it's private, not open to the public. The neighborhood
is outside the center city, an area where young families set up hopeful
households in the late 1920s and early 1930s. Streets named for poets,
three-storey stucco buildings. Cars are parked all along both sides of
the street. You can hear TVs, dogs, birds, children playing. Occasionally a bike rider glides past. I wonder if it was as leafy sixty years ago.
There should be plaques on houses throughout Europe: A Jew lived
here and was taken away.

Anne was four when they left in 1933; Margot was six.

Perhaps Margot remembered:

"Frankfurt, the house, the neighborhood, the protected feeling of it,
safe, bright, like in the country, but the excitement, too, the newness
of it. The best of everything, said my mother: Brand-new sturdy outside, delicate antiques inside. In Amsterdam, we learned to see verti-
cally, to look up and down. All is narrow and the streets are crooked
and thin. Contained. I was sorry to move away from everything familiar. From my native language. Everything in Amsterdam is approximate. And old. Compare and contrast. In Amsterdam we find
what is already here. Someone else has already named everything.
Anne, I don't think, really understands what is happening. We
brought our old grandfather clock with us here, because it too is tall
and thin. Ticks like a soft heartbeat, brooding over us."

Perhaps Margot grieved:

"July 1942. To leave yet again another house, in Amsterdam. They
have named me. The Nazis have found me. They know I am here. A
post card ordering me to pack my winter clothes and appear for a
transport to Germany. Instead I left the house, rode my bicycle with
Miep to what became the Annex. Rain protected us; no one stopped
us. And we arrived. I was the first one in the family to enter it that day.
The boxes were already there. Night fell.

"July 1943. Over time I grew quieter and quieter, they said. My
thoughts raged inside then slowed. Everything slowed. I followed

the course for French, for shorthand. At night we went downstairs to
file and alphabetize for the company – for its benefit, for ours, a slender thread connecting us to the real world, commerce.

"We could not get away from the chime of the Westertoren clock,
every quarter hour. It surprised me each time; nothing seemed pre-
dictable about it. I missed the steady ticking of our clock at home,
imagined it slowing down to match the winding down of my
thoughts. My stomach throbbed, my head. My heartbeat pounded
in code: It is time to die. That's why I was so quiet, in order to hear
the heart's message. I couldn't tolerate Anne's chatter. I abhorred
singing."

Margot also didn't write:

"Of the day they came for us, August 4, 1944. It was late morning,
happened fast. I gathered some bread, a Bible, a threadbare sweater –
buttons missing. We tramped out, like machines set in motion. The
sun hit us for a moment before we were herded into the car. Silent, of
course, on the way to the station. Anne couldn't bear to look out the
window. I did. Hungry for the familiar but impersonal landmarks.
Signs in Dutch and German. German, the language we no longer
memorized. Everyone was thin. But their hair shone. Wind riffled
through skirts. That's what we'd been missing: the benign unpredict-
ability of the breeze.

"You can imagine the rest."

AT BERGEN-BELSEN, WINTER 1945

Margot ran out of language. Everything seeped from her. She was
barely eighteen. Her name appeared on lists of people who didn't
come back. The day of death unmarked. She left no papers behind
that were gathered up and stored in a file drawer in a *maison de commerce* in Amsterdam, then translated, published. Of her family, only
her father came *de retour*. The Annex is now a *musée*. It is a center for
l'éducation, to search for *la cause*. Margot has lost her *envie*. It no
longer matters if it is *aprés-demain* or *avant-hier*, she has lost today,
the glue that binds one minute to the next, as once marked by the
German-made grandfather clock. Her *sang* is as dry as *poudre à canon*.
Time is the *voleur*. She offers no *conseil*. This is not her bouquet.

Eating Horse

What happened was he joined the cavalry but he forgot. And he put on a uniform to ride his horse but he forgot. And he ate his meals with the rest of the men but he forgot. And he slept in barracks or on the ground for many nights but he forgot. And he worked with military men who herded Salonikan Jews to their deaths but he – .

He said he was in the city working on his dissertation at the time.

And when the researchers reminded him about his life, he said he'd forgotten. He had erased it from his memory, from the lines and creases in his body, his muscles, his bones. And he, Kurt Waldheim, cried to the heavens, to his assembled accusers: I forgot!

Or to be more precise, at first he said, This isn't true, and then he said, It's true these things happened, but by the hands of others, I didn't know about it.

And a political opponent, usually so discreet, a nod here, a grunt here, a slight shake of the head, who had refused to enter the fray, finally said, Kurt Waldheim wasn't a Nazi, his horse was.

Allowing himself a guffaw.

That was all the artist needed. The artist was a man named Alfred Hrdlicka, a last name as non-German as, say, Waclawik, which was the original surname of Kurt Waldheim's father. The artist Hrdlicka went to his studio and made a ten-foot-tall wooden horse. He put a Nazi cap on the horse and took it to rallies and festivals, wherever the president addressed crowds. He even took it to the Vatican. The artist called his work a monument against forgetfulness.

Or else groups of artists and intellectuals built the horse. Depends on what you read. Some news reports said that protesters made giant horses out of papier-mâché. So the horses would be light – easy to carry, an important attribute of things to take to rallies. Prêt-à-porter.

And the furor died down and other dramas took its place.

§

Do you remember whether Waldheim was reelected? Do you remember whether he was allowed back in the U.S.? Do you remember if there was a boycott against Austria?

Do you remember the protests over Bitburg?

Do you remember wooden horses? Do you remember how to make papier-mâché? Papier-mâché is made from newspaper. You can tear the front page into strips, soak the strips in water and flour, drape them over a balloon to make a piñata. When the piñata's dry, you can tear a small hole in it and pour in candy and prizes. Then cover the hole, cover your eyes, and turn in circles and hit the piñata with a stick. Until the chocolates come tumbling out.

    Do you remember breaking the piñata at birthday parties?

    Do you remember candies collected in bags at Halloween?

    Do you remember Trick or Treat for UNICEF?

When Kurt Waldheim left New York as U.N. secretary-general, he took the silver from his U.N. residence and tried to take the furniture, too. We don't remember that. All we remember was that he was connected with the United Nations, that utopian body, like the late Dag Hammarskjöld, man from a neutral, pleasant, snowy country. Let's name a plaza after Waldheim, too.

Ring the bell. Don't go inside unless you know the family. X-ray the apples for razors; the local hospital does it for free.

    This Halloween don't dress up as a former secretary-general. Don't dress either as a former secretary-general's horse, a German-speaking Mr. Ed. *Herr Ed, der Nazi.* (Tune in to reruns right after *Hogan's Heroes*.) Don't dress like a horse, besides it's hard to be a whole horse by yourself, with legs much longer than your arms. If it's history you want, dress as a Greek warrior, a marathoner. Or a beautiful woman, the most beautiful throughout time – Helen of Troy, a face that launched a thousand ships. Ships of war that led to the Trojan horse. A horse on wheels with Greek warriors inside. The Trojans' curiosity got the better of them and so they rolled the huge hollow wooden horse inside their walls.

Which is not the story of Kurt Waldheim. He went to war and worked in intelligence and supplies for Hitler's Army Group E, which made its mark on Salonika and Montenegro. The group, say the researchers, dealt savagely with partisans and deported forty thousand Jews to Auschwitz. Waldheim recorded all this in an official journal. A good secretary even then. After the war his commander was hanged as a war criminal. So it is better to throw away the military jacket and instead dress as Helen, be beautiful. Wear gold coins around your waist. If the coins are chocolate, you can eat them later.

The artist Hrdlicka who built the wooden horse had been commissioned to make a monument in Vienna, to the war dead. He made it of granite and marble. It shows a Jew scrubbing the streets. This is what Jews did the day of the Anschluss, in 1938, when Germany "invaded" Austria, as more than half a million Viennese cheered.

Hrdlicka's sculpture stands on grassy Albertinaplatz. Buried underneath the greenery are bodies of Viennese killed by Allied bombs. But don't think about that; nearby are what Vienna prefers to be known for: the Sacher Hotel, the Albertina museum, the opera house.

Have you ever had a Sacher torte? It is made of layers: chocolate cake and apricot jam. Have you ever seen the miniatures at the Albertina? Have you ever heard *Der Ring des Nibelungen*? It debuted at the Vienna Opera, according to my Britannica.

Have you ever danced the waltz?

§

Perhaps you've wondered what happens to a person after he becomes internationally non grata.

Does he lie low, raging to his intimates? Or confess, scourge himself, do good works? Or sit under a tree and dream of the olden days, when Austria was the first name of an empire, when its reach extended from Prague to Lvov to Sarajevo, when a small-town boy could, by dint of fanatic hard work, make his mark on the world?

Imagine this instead: Helmut Kohl invites him to lunch. Austria issues a stamp in his honor. He is knighted by the pope.

§

After World War I, Communists tried to take control of the new republic. In April 1919 revolutionaries killed five policemen and wounded an officer's horse. The horse fell to the ground. A mob surrounded it, fighting – over pieces of horsemeat. The members of the crowd clutched their spoils and ran home to cook their horsey Easter dinners.

They were starving.

But they were not alone in eating horse. The triumphant Allies, living in the Hotel Sacher, ate the imperial cavalry. How do we know? A horse butcher sued for an unpaid bill – two thousand crowns. The conquerors ate the enemies' horses.

§

The taste of horse, you imagine, is deep and dark, gamey, bloody, tougher than beef. Perhaps it has a distinctive smell. But your dogs eat it, the dogs whom you kiss on the lips. It tastes good to them, natural. It's dinner. They wag their tails for it, whimper in impatience. You buy it ground and reshaped, packed in pressed cellophane inside bright boxes with pictures of happy dogs on the front. It's easy to forget where it comes from.

THE ONES YOU
BREAK BREAD WITH

1. CHICAGO: WINTER 1995

Seth, nearly eight, falls off his chair. Again. His father warns him: "Twenty minutes." Meaning: twenty minutes' time out when they get home. Jesse, his twin, sits across from Seth, next to me at Café Avanti, in our neighborhood. Their mother is at a brunch. One boy orders a square of cold pizza, the other, hot. The father and I, old friends, eat the discards: mushrooms, broccoli.

"Dad, are your eyes blue?" asks Jesse.

His father, Barry, widens his very brown eyes behind his wire-rims. All of us have brown eyes. As does their mother. Seth is reading *Maus*, Art Spiegelman's nonfiction comic book about the Holocaust. The Jews are portrayed as mice, Poles are pigs, and Nazis are cats. It's in two volumes. He has the first one.

"Do they know what it's about?" I ask Barry.

"Yes," he says. "I let them read any literature as long as it's good."

They know they are Jewish, though at home they have a small lighted tree on a front windowsill. Every December their mother, my friend Sharon, makes latkes, every Passover she grinds her own whitefish for gefilte fish for her seder. The famous question asked again and again on that holiday: "Why is this night different?" All is answered by the end.

Today, on this Sunday in January, Jesse, absorbing the content of his brother's book so matter-of-factly, asks us if Hitler had blond hair.

"Dark," I say.

"Do you know what he looked like?" he asks.

"He had brown hair and a little mustache," I say.

"Did Hitler kill all the English?" asks Seth.

"He bombed England," I say. "It was called the Blitz. I know someone who remembers it."

"Are we in the east or west?" asks Seth.

Jesse falls off his chair. They are pliable, Saint Bernard puppies in down coats, playing too roughly with the sweetener packets at the center of the table. Jesse is writing in his journal, about Teddy, who is either a bear or a boy. Their mother is red-headed, small, she could pass. These boys are not quiet. They are creatures made to roll in the snow, to bounce down stairs, to smear Sweet 'N Low on the tables of coffeehouses in their neighborhood. Their parents make them write in their journals daily. The boys complain about this. I tell them about Colette: "A French writer whose husband locked her in a room so that she would write."

Seth chews off his eraser, looks up from *Maus* to put pencil shavings in his mouth.

How are the pigs of *Maus* different from Power Rangers, or from last year's Ninja Turtles? Next Halloween, will the boys dress up as small white mice in striped rags, begging candy at the doors of neighbors, indifferent to the presence or absence of mezuzahs, the rectangle that Jews nail to their doorposts? There's a mezuzah at their door. Sharon would pass as Gentile. Her coloring is fair, she is able to flirt, a nervous woman nonetheless possessing sangfroid. I am dark – dark brown eyes and hair – tongue-tied, tongue thickening when faced with authority. I could see Sharon smuggling pistols in Occupied Poland, running to board trains to deliver ration and ID cards, shaking, vowing never to do it again, and making the return trip, and the next, the story more harrowing in each retelling. I admire the fierce way she plays tennis.

Barry, a short Allen Ginsberg, there would be no hope for him. Though many of the obvious-looking Jews survived, the darkest, the frailest. That is the riddle that goes beyond history, beyond DNA. And he is clever, nonparochial, grew up among the Scandinavians of Minnesota, does not naturally seek his own kind. Indifferent to the holidays of his tribe. Got his poetry published in an anthology of Polish writing because of the land his ancestors once lived in, were confined to. Yiddish speakers who for a moment lived among Poles. Presumably without full citizenship, without portfolio.

We are writers hungry for publication. The boys are hungry for adventure. I grab at my history, at the stream, the tribe I call my people. Barry reminisces about his life before they were born, but says now, "They're so cute it's worth it."

Jesse wants a special clock for his birthday for games of speed chess. Barry hopes they'll be yuppies – "Be a stockbroker," he says – so they won't be impoverished writers. I have known them for seven years and still cannot tell them apart. That is my secret. I wait until they are named, addressed in conversation. Seth slips again from his chair.

Surprising myself with my patience, my calm voice, perhaps dipping into my pacifist past: "Let's get the chair out of the way so people can pass through." One boy cries over his drink. I ask again and again, "Which juice drink did you want if not this one?"

Barry exchanges Breakfast Surprise for Juice Squeeze.

"Mango in it," says Seth in despair.

Their grandparents live in other Midwest cities. Their community does not include bakers or tailors with numbers on their arms. It is early 1995. Chicago is the capital of the world in exporting used brick. A few dry leaves hang curled from the branches of trees. Snow has melted but still we need to bundle up. Tomorrow is Martin Luther King's birthday. Tonight is Tu B'Shevat, the birthday of the trees.

How could we confine these boys to an attic, a coal shed, a compartment in a hayloft? To bits of bread for years on end as we await the end of the war? Would I die for these boys? Would I protect them with my body? Why are we not given these choices? Why are we the lucky ones who are given the choice of not having to make these choices?

The newspapers report of eight year olds who care for their younger siblings, who are lookouts for dealers, who die in crossfire. Who die when government protective agencies do not separate them fast enough from their parents. Their death is a public matter. The cameras pan across the grieving family, the newspapers print, say, the Easter Sunday pictures of the boy who didn't have a chance to join Little League, the girl who was so helpful to her mother. Somehow it's important to learn their names. The *Tribune*, aching for a Pulitzer, once did a year-long series on children who died. Every day: body count, photos, Johnny we hardly knew ye. After a year, the *Trib* stopped counting.

2. CHICAGO, MORE WINTER 1995

I've always said I didn't want children. The responsibility, the time, the way they take over your life.

Now I have just met a man who wants them.

I walk the three blocks from my apartment (brick, wood floors, silver-painted radiators) to Barry and Sharon's one-hundred-year-old house. In their dining room – shiny wood table, air-conditioning unit covered with embroidered cloth from Israel, nearby big jars of beans and grains – I tell them about this man I'll call Ted. Whom I am seeing. As tentative and ambiguous as it sounds. A man who wants it all – wife, family, house. A Jewish man, friend of a friend, who drives impatiently and too often a too-expensive car with a phone in it. Works out in the fanciest club in town.

He lives in a glassy condo with long pale hallways and black and white rooms. There is little warmth there, no nod to an earlier century, to home-spun materials. In Barry and Sharon's three-story wooden house, I run free with my critique. I have met the marketing-industrial complex and it is Ted. I do not approve. But there are sparks. Sharon takes it as a good sign that we spar. Redeeming: he has a therapy practice of his own.

§

At dinner in a Japanese restaurant we both like, I tell Ted about the twins and sugar packets and *Maus*. Will he take this as a sign I do want children after all? Probably not; I imagine that he sees me as I see myself: childlike, childish, not a potential parent. He speaks of a couple he knows who seems blessed: three lovely children. He says his friend's child will hug him, and that he says to this child, "Give me a kiss," and he does.

I am proud that I have said to Barry and Sharon, "If the boys don't want to kiss me good-bye, it's fine." I believe in giving choices. I remember what it is like to be a child, to have to reach for the light switch, to know the painful limits of the body, the choices it keeps you from having. "Children having children," you always read in the headlines and commentaries but the writers mean the poor, the dark, at twelve and fourteen, the ones who do not read or send faxes or poetry out into the world. They do not mean childish women like me, who thrill themselves to sleep with tales of evil in our century, who eat richly flavored ice cream from the carton, who light their doorways with colored lights, receive wind-up toys from friends for birthdays.

Ted believes in seriousness, has hung black and white photos, framed in black, on the walls of his condo. The other walls are glass – windows that let him see the city at a distance, are cleaned, perhaps, as part of his maintenance fee.

How tantalizing to see everything, and thus think you should be able to understand it.

From this box he makes appointments to ask consumers: Would you want this? Or this? What if it were this way instead? What are you looking for in – ?

Over his bed is the famous photo by Robert Doisneau of the passion-kiss I always thought was on the way to or from the war. Across from the Doisneau is a black-and-white photo of a languid nude woman partly enclosed in a box. Ted likes to ask people how they feel about the picture; some are disturbed by it, he tells me, smiling and waiting. His own personal Rorschach.

I'm not sure what I think. I don't feel much when I see it; it reminds me of a conversation in Tom Stoppard's *Rosencrantz and Guildenstern are Dead*. In the play Rosencrantz tells Guildenstern that people can't imagine what it would be like to be dead in a box because we can only imagine what it would be like to be alive in one. It shouldn't bother us to be dead in a box because we wouldn't feel the box, we'd be dead.

At least, says Rosencrantz, if you're alive inside the box, you can keep hoping that someone will tell you to come out.

It's the waiting to be summoned that strikes me. Waiting to be rescued. For someone to call your name, redeem you, guide you out of the darkness, let you emerge.

Death stands in all our margins. One night Ted mentions a family tragedy. I struggle to say the right thing, think, So he has known sorrow I can't imagine. He has trusted me with this. For this I am grateful. But don't know him well enough to provide true comfort.

§

When the twins come to my house, they roll on the floor, complain about the spiciness of the food, twirl the plastic blades of the un-plugged fan. I have almost grown to love them. When I visit my five-year-old niece in Texas, she tells me she loves me. Is that training? Is that mirroring? Because I am part of her family, flesh of her flesh, blood? Blood and body, the true religion of the Jewish people? Com-munion with family, the deepest heart of the religion, the time-river-soul of it?

§

The last time I was in love, Ted says, the two of us fought each other so hard, each in order to be right all the time.

Being right was proof of his existence, his right to exist. To be right and alone.

Once I saw a play about Gramsci, the Italian political philosopher. This is what I remember from it: that he was the perfect man of the left, the synthesizer, always looking for the third way. He softened all desires, molded them into a movement, believed in meeting not just halfway, but in a new place, unknown, frightening to both sides. He was jailed. He wrote letters to his wife from prison.

Perhaps that's the only place from which to write love letters, the way that foxholes are the best chapels of all. You must give up what you believe, what you think makes you *you*, to plunge into/fall into/ embrace the third way, which isn't me or Ted or the patterns we have grown into living each day but the possibility we don't know yet, the thing we haven't seen, the children not yet conceived.

3. CHICAGO: THE APPEARANCE OF SPRING, 1995

You would think, now, that Ted and I are involved, that we settled it, are entwined, happy. You would think that. This story is true – is it not? – nonfiction, not made up. Each part is true, as well as I can re-member, which twin said what, as far as I can tell; and details down to the gray shadows in the Doisneau, reproduction of reproduction. Just as that French couple eventually came up for air, disengaged, stopped looking at one another, first for an instant, then longer, be-cause the world is so large. Became aware of themselves. The photographer captures a true moment. Several. And does not close the shutter at other true moments.

But alas, there were awkward moments, unhappy moments, judgmental and uncomfortable times.

4. HOUSTON: SPRING 1995/5755

Most Jews go to Passover seders. At least, American Jews. A survey I read said eighty-six percent of families made up of Jews only (Jews are almost always counted in families) go to seders. I am part of that majority; I flew on two planes to Texas, Easter weekend too, feeling like the only Jew on the plane, as I always do when going to Texas for Jewish holidays. As if I should have a tag on me, as children under a certain age do: Please deliver her to Jews. As if I were on a mission of God. I was; in keeping with superstition, I carried a dollar for charity, to give to the first person who asked at my destination. I learned this from my mother's family – God will not strike you down – i.e., let your plane crash – if you're on an errand of mercy.

It's worked so far.

Houston is green and humid, bursting with purple azaleas and white crape myrtle, lizards rustling through bushes. Palm trees stand in some yards and on esplanades; pansies, a winter flower in East Texas, are still in bloom. Everyone I know here lives in low-slung houses built in the 1950s and 1960s.

My second day in town, I go to visit my cousin, in Houston to see her stepfather Otto. It's perhaps the last time I'll be in that house. My aunt died a month before, and Otto's already put the house on the market. He asks me, "Why do so many people like seders?"

"Because," I say, "they are do-it-yourself. They're at home. It's family."

"Yes, family," he agrees. "Family is the reason."

He used to come to our seders and laugh at our singing. His voice is melodious, his English richly accented; he left Berlin just before Kristallnacht, settled with his family in Texas, knowing the words to the state song and phrases from the Sears catalog. He served in the U.S. Army and liberated a small camp in Germany, the inmates hesitating before trusting the young German-speaker, who did not know Yiddish.

My cousin Dinah tells me: A commemoration program is planned on concentration camp liberation. Otto was invited to talk. Part of the program, he was told, would include *Hatikvah*, the Israeli national anthem, but not *The Star-Spangled Banner*. Otto made this proposition: Either black me out of the program or insert the anthem.

The anthem will be sung, she said. (I find out later it was not.)

At the front of the house he is selling there's a holder for a flagpole; he displays the American flag on appropriate occasions. His first wife also came from Germany, also settled in Texas. His second wife, my aunt, died in late February after what seemed like a series of strokes. A native Texan. A late-in-life blonde who laughed a lot. Who volunteered a lot, with Otto – visiting the sick, welcoming Soviet refugees, helping in a clothing pantry. Less than a week after her death (a quick and earlier trip home for me) Otto was already collecting her eyeglasses to donate to charity, urging my cousin to box up her college memorabilia. "Otto the Hun," jokes my cousin.

"Opposites worked for twenty-three years," said Otto, "different strokes for different folks."

"Don't say 'strokes,'" said my cousin.

In Houston cousins abound. After our seder I visit another cousin's house. I'll call her Debra. By the time I arrive, most of her guests have left. Two of her sons sit at the long half-empty table, entranced with Game Boys. The youngest falls off his chair. But only once. He's a fourth grader, round-faced, sweet-faced, not a cherub – but almost, looking tonight like a premature businessman in crisp white shirt, dark pants. I'll call him Michael.

He has a mouth. He's the kind of kid who would shout (with glee) that the emperor was naked, and more, that his dick (that was the word he'd use) was hanging out, his fat jiggling, ridiculous. In fact he talks of his grandmother, who died two years ago, how you couldn't tell whether she was smiling or not because of the fat on the sides of her face. "Like a bulldog," he says. He doesn't know the word "jowls" or he would use it. His mother excuses, or rather explains: "He said earlier how much he missed her." Here they speak of the dead the way they spoke of the living – no gilding of lilies here.

This young cousin is self-assured. A boy who knows his place. He is generally pleased with himself, but he's also likeable. This is a family pleased with itself, though not with its fate. After Debra's father then sister died, says Debra, they asked the funeral home if it gave volume discounts. A mutual cousin in her fifties died this week in Dallas. Fast – from a malignant brain tumor in January to cancer everywhere this spring.

At the seders we – those of us in our thirties and forties – attend, we note each year how the ranks of the middle-age are depleted (especially since the definition of middle-aged keeps stretching, away from ourselves). There are fewer and fewer of the older generation, the ones in their eighties and nineties. At our seder, there was only one old man at the table, my grandmother's cousin. He mumbled and caused my mother's lips to purse when she saw he was writing with a ballpoint pen on his white cloth napkin.

At Debra's seder, Michael says, nearly triumphant with the novelty of it, after he asked the traditional Four Questions, a member of the older generation asked: "Is anyone going to ask the Four Questions?"

Our great-aunt Ethel, on the other hand, is intact, chatty and bustling; whenever I see her she says how grateful she is for her half-dozen grandchildren, who call her often, always remember her birthday. She is the surviving sibling of seven, maybe, eight. Her brother, my grandfather, died in July, at ninety-four. Aunt Ethel is the only relative who still asks me, "When are you going to find a *khosn*?" At first I thought that was Yiddish for an upright (Jewish) man, but now I know it means a groom. I don't mind when she asks.

(Months after Ted and I have stopped speaking, I do meet a *khosn*, according to my first and wrong definition.)

The next day at a Passover brunch, an aunt (other side of the family) says she likes coming to town for happy occasions. The two times before this were for funerals. She says someone in the family needs to have a bar mitzvah, a wedding. My mother says maybe my aunt's grandsons will be the next to get married. The grandsons are in their early twenties. I am in the background, putting away chairs. I am a ghost. I don't exist. They are frightened to ask me, "When is your turn?" Because my turn is up, already taken, time to move over for the twenty-somethings? Because they have stopped hoping, wondering? They are afraid of offending me. No, they are afraid of hurting me.

§

My father died in 1991. My mother is alone. My aunt died in 1995. Her first husband died in the early 1970s. My brother-in-law's parents died in the late 1980s, after which my sister said, "Someone in this family needs to have a baby," and then she had her third child. The party for her baby's naming was bounteous – heart-shaped muffins, fat strawberries, flowers; it was time for a banquet. A feast.

My mother says, "When I'm old, just take me out to the woods and shoot me."

I try to make a joke: "You never liked the woods during Girl Scouts. We'll take you to the shopping mall and leave you."

She doesn't want to live to ninety-six, which is how old her mother is.

5. CHICAGO: COLD SPRING 1995

Spring weather and winter weather, back and forth, each day different. Sun is shining warmly and the radiators still clang. One day it's 40, the next day, 58, going down to 32. Misty and terrible wind. Today: bright, everyone on the street. Daffodils and red-yellow tulips, pink flowerings on magnolia trees, crocuses, pink and blue and white hyacinths in the little urban front yards in my neighborhood, even some feathery pink azaleas behind an iron fence.

My friend Mitch calls. He's the one who introduced me to Ted. Mitch tells me that Ted's father has cancer. It's especially hard because Ted is an only child. "It's not so bad when you've got your own family," Mitch says. Which is what Mitch wants to have, too. "Friends are not the same," he says. "Are your friends the same? Have you tested them?" he asks.

Knock wood, thank God – there has been no test. My friends and I substitute in each other's classes, borrow and lend cars (not often), babysit (not often), bring food to each other when we're sick, accompany one another to the hospital (the surgery is always minor), calm each other down when agitated about jobs/lovers/family (often).

This is not the cancer, the blood on your door, the call from headquarters, the sacrifice, the night watch, taking children as your own; not the world of passwords, underground cells, nights where you unquestioning, gladly, would give your last – drop of water, cyanide capsule, pistol, bullet – to your friend. We don't wonder, Would I give her away under torture?

No one knocks on the door asking to be hidden. No one knocks, either, asking any of us to round out a minyan.

Mitch asks, "Are there friends you could call if you didn't have a place to go for a holiday?" "Barry and Sharon," I said. Though there are holidays they don't celebrate. Every Passover I go to Texas, and on the High Holidays stay in Chicago and wrangle with my friend Dina over when and where we'll go to services. Mitch spent Passover with the family of his brother's new girlfriend. He lived overseas but moved back to Chicago to be around family. His mother is failing. He has come to my house for holiday dinners.

Yesterday I went to Sharon's to borrow an egg to make brownies for a Passover potluck. (I hardly ever use eggs; the last dozen I bought sat in the refrigerator for eight months before I threw them out.) She asked if I wanted to take back with me my big dictionary, on permanent loan since 1990, when I left town for a year.

I was afraid I'd have trouble balancing both the egg and dictionary. "Another time," I said. She walked me down the stairs, got on her bike. The daffodils in her yard were in a row, nodding, her tomatoes and broccoli not yet planted for the summer. She moved a big branch that had somehow been struck down.

I told her about a high school program I'd heard about, where each kid is given a raw egg to take care of for a week. It's supposed to teach them how much trouble it is to take care of a baby.

She said it sounded like a good idea. Then she rode away on her bike, the one still holding a child seat.

This is our life, each minute of it, tying to the next. The phone rings. We get it or wait for voice mail to claim it. We talk. We tell the truth or not. We live inside of history, but make the choice to grab and wrestle with it or leave our hands slack, open. We see the big-eyed children in magazines asking for monthly stipends. We turn the page or not. We smile noncommittally at a neighbor on a porch step. We look for lovers. We're asked, "What's new?" We answer, "This and this and that, not much."

Or, "Much." Is it just time, is it just the time we spend that builds these small filaments, from one person to the next?

"Do you want to come over and see *Triumph of the Will*?" asks Mitch. "I don't have time," I say. "But I'd like to."

"Do you want to come for dinner in three weeks?" Sharon asks. "And tonight? And can my friend Lew stay at your house while you're gone?"

"Will you come and pick up your fax that's been lying on my floor for three days?"

"Will your boys eat Indian food if I don't make it too spicy?"

"Will you tell me what you thought of my story?"

"Would you like the mushrooms on my salad?"

How easy it is to offer food I'm not planning to eat. Let's not think of want, let's stay in the world of bounty, where we leave generous tips at neighborhood cafés (today I'm with Sharon at the Mozart Café) where the music is always classical. We're in no hurry – the papers we're grading aren't due for another few days. Sharon leaves the café first, gets on her bike. I stay behind, not watching as she rides away on her ten-speed, and I'm not bothering to watch her disappear down the sidewalk. I take it for granted that I'll see her again.

6. CHICAGO, SKOKIE: MORE WINTER, MORE SPRING 1995

Mitch's mother is losing her memory, minute by minute. He reads to her and she understands but doesn't remember from one day to the next. The book he reads to his mother every day in Skokie is *Mila 18*, about the Jewish ghetto resistance. His father was in Auschwitz and Bergen-Belsen, his mother was drifting through Poland on her own, twelve years old, and then surrendered herself at a work camp. The camp didn't have a name, he says, or else he never heard it. Late at night, on the phone, I ask Mitch questions, write down his answers: "We always knew. At first I think it was just a mystery. I knew that the Germans were bad and that there was some like dark place that my parents came from which was Europe. And I don't remember hearing particular stories. Except my grandparents were all dead. My friends had grandparents. I had many uncles and aunts. I didn't realize my parents had accents until eighth grade and friends started making fun of them. They used to speak Yiddish all the time. To hide what they were saying from us. I found that obnoxious even when I was a little kid. I made my mother promise for my fifth birthday that she would translate. I thought you could buy a translating box because I saw one on television."

He felt like a stranger in this country, an outsider, outside of the lives of other Jewish Americans. He doesn't feel entitled because his parents didn't feel entitled. But I feel the same way, I say, and my parents were born in this country. Is it from having asthma all my life, or from growing up Jewish in Texas, or from the inexplicable – psychological makeup, luck of the draw?

"Are you a victim without a Holocaust?" Mitch asks me, joking: "Victims in search of a Holocaust." I know he's thinking of Pirandello's *Six Characters in Search of an Author*. The characters were set loose in the world, on the stage, looking for a strong hand to guide them. They were lost, trapped in their narratives – or fate. They couldn't change, they didn't have new stories to build and live inside. So they roamed, argued, irate that they had been misplaced like so many handkerchiefs or socks, that no one longed to hear what they had to say to each other, to follow the drama they were fated to perform.

In Hebrew school we saw films of the camps. All I remember are grainy images on a small screen. On Passover, my father would talk about "our brethren" still in the Soviet Union and those who had died in Europe in the war. He felt that connection: There but for fortune . . .

Four or so months have passed and I don't remember the feel of Ted, or am not sure – maybe I do recall the solidity of his body. I mention the Doisneau photo to friends and they tell me there was a recent controversy over it. I look it up. In 1993 Doisneau admitted that that famous photo, "The Kiss at City Hall" – snapped in 1950 – was staged.

The next year, he died in Paris, after a heart bypass operation. He was eighty-one.

In my quest for accuracy, I look through a volume of Gramsci's letters; I can't quite find the passion I remember from the play, the letters to his wife are not filled with declarations of love. Maybe my definition of "love letter" is too literal.

Months later I run into the black-and-white photograph of a sailor kissing a nurse on V-J Day in Times Square. Aha! That's the World War II photo I had in mind. The photographer was Alfred Eisenstaedt. A real nurse. A real sailor. A real end to the war: August 14, 1945.

§

One night this year, or maybe the end of last – snowy, winter – I walked to Barry and Sharon's for dinner. It was dark and their little house was nestled in such a cozy-looking way, cheery and perfect as New England, that I felt comforted, cosseted, even, by the sight. I stood before their front steps and said to myself, I will look back at this moment, this warmth, and feel nostalgic. And pine for it. And then I felt sad, as if I'd already absorbed the loss. I went up the steps and inside I said to them: I was feeling so sad for this moment in retrospect, when it will be gone and I'll miss it. I was grasping, grasping to keep things as they were, to keep the balance from shifting. But grateful I could tell them about my anticipatory fear.

And then we talked and drank and had dinner and talked more and probably laughed, I don't remember exactly, and I left when it got late and walked home, past the dark and shuttered baseball stadium, the boxy little neighborhood fire station, the corner bars, and other three-story red brick apartment houses with wooden floors and molding, filled with couches, chairs, rugs, paintings, posters, beds, dishes, plants, books, computers, cabinets, tablecloths, futons, nightstands and other things we collect in order to anchor us in the world we want to believe is permanent.

7. CHICAGO: JANUARY 31, 2001

Mitch's mother has died and his father has remarried; Mitch reports that Ted is married. Summer 1995 I met my true love, my *khosn*. Two years ago I moved from my apartment to a condo, two blocks closer to Barry and Sharon. Three friends have survived breast cancer. Two others have died of it. Barry has multiple sclerosis and walks with a cane. Sometimes the little rubber tip falls off. Café Mozart has gone out of business. Café Avanti has, as one of the *baristas* said, changed owners. Sharon no longer has the little tree in the front window at Christmastime. The first night in my new place, a Friday, my lover and I went for take-out Thai. We invited Barry and Sharon and the boys over and in an unusual move for us, celebrated the Sabbath: lit candles, blessed the wine and challah. We all sat on the floor to eat our (decidedly nonkosher) pad thai and shrimp curry. Then they left because the boys were singing that night in the temple choir. They joined the synagogue a couple of years ago so the boys could become bar mitzvah. The b'nai mitzvah was in June 2000. They postponed the date once, because in October 1999 Jesse was diagnosed with cancer. It hasn't been difficult to help out, for any of us.

When his hair grew back he dyed it blue and said it was from the chemo. Seth had dyed his hair, then grew it out, and cultivated a Mohawk. Jesse was in remission from April until late October 2000. His doctor called him "Mr. Side Effects" because it seemed he got every one. They were especially bad the second time around, in December 2000 and January. He grew thin and wasn't able to eat. Doctors tried to manage the pain.

I got to know him better over the past year and a half. He asked me how I could be atheist but still celebrate Jewish holidays. I heard him tell a nurse that the Nazis would have killed him because they experimented on twins. Three days ago on the couch at his house we watched *Mary Poppins* on TV and he noted that the mother was for women's rights but was a housewife. We agreed that Julie Andrews was nothing like the austere character in the book. Yesterday he and his father watched *A Clockwork Orange* on DVD and when Marlene, his public school tutor, came over, they discussed reform and rehabilitation. When he was in the hospital in November he asked medical personnel whom they had voted for and challenged the Republicans. He enjoyed reading the satiric *Onion* newspaper and the *New York Times*, and appreciated the humor and commentary of George Carlin and Chris Rock. He won the school spelling bee last year but couldn't compete further because he was in the hospital.

His favorite Winnie the Pooh character was Tigger, and his favorite doctor in the hospital gave him a stuffed Tigger. Jesse liked to have his back and hands and feet rubbed with vanilla-scented lotion. The morphine made him itch all over and when I rubbed the lotion on his back yesterday I could feel the cuts where he had scratched himself. When I rubbed his back, I felt connected to him, the way you feel connected to someone through sex, but it was not sexual. It was be-yond words. Maybe it is the way a mother feels bound to her child.

Jesse suffered but did not like to be called brave. He thought it more apt to say that he had "put up with" a lot.

Last night the favorite doctor and a nurse-practitioner came by the house and Jesse and Seth delighted in the doctor's card tricks. We all got on the nurse's case because she's a Republican. Later that night Jesse made his way unsteadily upstairs to bed. At 5:30 A.M., holding his mother's hand, he died.

In the Mother Tongue

"Shulamis," the teacher says, as I knew she would, "vos hert zikh?"

Shulamis is my Yiddish name and the Yiddish teacher is asking what's being heard, meaning, "What's doing?" The class nearly always begins this way, round-robin, like group therapy, like consciousness-raising. It's all female, it so happens, though men have come and gone, mostly gone. Over the years of weeks, we've learned of *tsores* – trouble – with contractors, computer repairmen, auto mechanics, and adult children; births, deaths, and illness; weddings and bar mitzvahs attended; cruises and other travels; and often, current movies and plays. Since I saw a performance Saturday night, I say just that, except that I say "forshung" instead of "forshtelung," which means I attended a research, rather than a play. Once that's cleared up, the teacher asks, "And what was it called?"

I improvise: "*Di Vagina Monologn.*"

I'm in luck: double cognates. But because our teacher doesn't want us to rely on cognates, she teaches us another word: *dos muterort*, mother place. Of course we have to ask why a vagina is neuter (*dos*) and the teacher reminds us that "beard" in Yiddish is feminine: *di bord*. She also tells us the Sanskrit word for vagina, "yoni." I continue with my recital. I tell them that the writer was the performer, that she wore a *zhupke* (skirt, but I meant *kleyd*, a dress) and no shoes. For a moment, my fellow Yiddishists imagine that Eve Ensler performed topless.

The questions come at me thick and fast, in Yiddish and English:

"About vaginas?"

"What is there to say?"

"You can't talk about everything. That's private."

"Dos muterort," I say, "iz shtum," using the only word I can think of for "silent." I'm thinking of one form of the letter "alef," which is *shtum*, or "silent."

"And the breasts," a classmate asks, "they speak?"

"Yoh," I say.

"Could I write a monologue about my nose?"

"It wouldn't be very interesting."

"The writer," I say, "interviewed many women."

"About their vaginas?"

"What did she ask them?"

I approximate: "'If your vagina could wear something, what would it wear?'"

"You mean underwear?"

"Neyn," I say. It made so much sense inside the theater, Ensler with her perfect shiny bob of hair, listing the answers women gave her – taffeta dress, mink – though even then it was hard to imagine, because how can you dress a part of you that is a passageway? In that semidarkness, it was easier to make the metaphorical leap. I wanted to say, "It's like asking, 'If you were a tree, what kind would you be?'" but the conditional is so difficult.

The conversation veers away and back, during which the teacher tells us the word for "period" (*pekl*), and another student says that we've already learned it. But the rest of us are so forgetful that we deny learning anything until we've heard it ten times. It's tricky to keep up with this wanted-dead-or-alive language, which few of us actually use outside each ninety-minute session.

The class meets in the chapel of an Orthodox synagogue in Chicago, though the class is sponsored by a nonsectarian Jewish adult education organization, not the synagogue. We used to meet in the library of a nearby worn-out building before it changed hands and became an Indian center. This chapel has a *mekhitse*, the wall that separates men and women at prayer. We meet in the women's section, not because the group happens to be all-female, but because there's more space to move around. In this room where we have learned there is no Yiddish word for "brunch" but there is one for "e-mail" (*blitz-post*), we now learn the words *damen-bandazh* (ladies-bandage), sanitary napkin; *klole*, (curse), and discuss whether God's curse was menstruation or childbirth.

After class, we walk down the synagogue hallway speaking (in English) about menstruation.

Later at home I look up "vagina" in my modern Yiddish-English dictionary (copyright 1968, reprinted 1990) and find *di vagina* [hard g] and *di mutersheyd*. (I trust my teacher, though; she gives us the most current translations.) I look for "tampon" (not there), "vulva" (missing), "clitoris" (gone), feeling uneasily like an eleven-year-old looking up dirty words in the dictionary. Does this mean that the folks who claim that Yiddish is dead are right, that the *mameloshn* – "mother tongue" – is not a living language? "Orgasm" (cognate) is listed, because, I assume, men have them. Same with "masturbation" (*der onanizm*). "Penis" is a cognate, and its slang variations, *shmuck* and *putz*, are unlisted but quite at home in America.

For a moment the bilingual dictionary makes me feel partially disappeared, my genitalia only half recognized. Later my teacher will tell me, via blitz-post, that there are about forty entries for "vagina" in her Yiddish thesaurus, and that her all-time favorite is *di mayse*, "the story." But before I know this, while I am still contemplating my too-empty dictionary, I think: For a few minutes, there we were – Orthodox and Conservative and secular Jewish women, hair covered and wildly uncovered – talking aloud and bilingually about vaginas as we sat by ourselves behind the mekhitse.

AMALEK

In Manhattan years ago, I wandered into a bookstore, made my way to the Judaica section. I picked up a book – I don't remember the title. That book told me this: Some Jews go through a ritual when using a new pen. They write the word Amalek and cross it out.

Amalek was the godson of Esau. Amalek was the ultimate enemy, reborn in each generation, who tried to strike out the Jews. Amalek must be made and struck out, before going on to new words.

I learned of this custom in the aisle of a bookstore run by a chain while on a visit to New York – not at the dinner table in Houston where I grew up, not in a synagogue in Chicago where I live; I learned of this homely custom hundreds of miles away from my home. By chance, and alone.

My parents never mentioned Amalek. But they were always looking over their shoulders. Only a fool, said my father, is happy all the time.

We are all making marks against Amalek, against our own annihilation. We write Amalek in our own terms. We cross it out in our own hand.

At a Yom Kippur service once, we wrote our sins on paper and released them, to float and fade in water.

Ashkenazi Jews give their babies the names of their dead. Each name is a statement against Amalek.

What if Amalek is just (boundariless, indiscriminate) death? What if he is shadow, familiar as our own bodies?

Jews are accustomed to being chosen. Without Amalek, our particular Amaleks, there is no history. We are used to our holidays – eating the sweet *charoset* to remind us of the mortar used by Jewish slaves, munching the tricornered pastry resembling the hat of Haman, who tried to kill the Jews of Persia.

After the death of masses we cling to individual voice and spirit, we believe again in capitalism. We publish books of Holocaust children's drawings, amazing to us because they are so much like other children's drawings. We become a collective again in order to mourn.

§

Somewhere in the synagogue in Houston is a prayer book dedicated to the memory of my father's father. I am named for him, same initials. About ninety years ago he arrived in Macon, Georgia, almost straight from the shtetl, the small Eastern European Jewish village – that mythical place of kindliness, splintery houses, charming accents, beards and rags.

I yearn for that ghetto, those neighbors, that life without telephones – the shtetl, my version of pastoral. Look, Ma, is that a fiddler on the roof?

§

I worshipped my father, says my father, for his cheerfulness in the face of adversity.

I have this on tape. My father is driving us around his old neighborhood in Houston, my recorder running.

Does depression run in your family? I ask.

No, he says, we're optimistic, cheerful, outgoing.

Then why am I so melancholy? I ask him.

Because you're very sensitive, he says. This is not a family trait, he tells me – it is mine, only mine.

I change the subject. What did your father tell you about the Old Country? I ask.

He told me he was glad to be gone.

§

My grandmother used to say that our family had *yikhes* – status, pedigree – that we are descended from the Vilna Gaon, the genius of Vilna, the town once known as the Jerusalem of Lithuania.

Now, golden Vilna is called Vilnius, another capital city that has lost its Jews. We Jews have learned to live without Vilna.

We are learning to live with Amalek, to raise our faces to the darkness of his vision and strike this Amalek. He is everything that will swallow us up. We are like Jonah alone in the great fish, who is filled with fears – that he will become the fish, that on land he will be forgotten. We fear no one will mourn us so we mourn ourselves first and remember this Amalek and make a strike through his name, make a mark that will lead us to our own.

§

In a hospital in Houston my father dies before my eyes. The rabbi recites the Twenty-third Psalm; doctors and nurse watch and unhook my father from machines. My uncle's hand is on my shoulder.

My father dies and returns in dreams where it is a secret that he is still alive. He tells me that I am living in his skin. Barefoot, in blue and white pajamas, he has returned not because he still cares about this life, but because he is faithful to the feeling he remembers he once had.

Amalek, he says, is not darkness or Other. It is a marker of separation, a name resurrected as a reminder not to forget, and above all . . . empty, he says.

He repeats it slowly – empty – knowing that is not the right word, wanting to stay to find the right one, wanting to remember why it matters.

Juggling: The New Year

Great thing for the family to do together, culture the kids can enjoy, it's a parking meter holiday, there's no traffic, we can bring Grandma, perfect – you could almost hear the parents thinking as they and their children tumbled into the Chicago Theatre on New Year's Day. The kids were in fancy red velvet dresses, Pokemon t-shirts, rompers for the too-young-to-sit-through-a-movie set, shiny Minnie Mouse shoes – and they were going to sit in the dark with their parents and guardians and be mesmerized by an ancient art with a few modern touches.

"There are hardly any other jugglers in the world who can do what he can do," a mother-sounding woman told a child seated next to her. They were in the row behind us. *Uh oh, I thought, it's already sounding force-fed, Art that's Good for You.* In front of us, taking up the whole row, was what appeared to be an extended family – grandmother, son, daughters and daughters-in-law, grandchildren. One of the adults was trying to convince a small boy that he should like red licorice or at least try it, the reason being that was what she had in hand. There was none of the preferred black licorice on sale out front.

Then it started. The juggler for the millennium, as he was billed in his punnily-titled show – "In Motion with Michael Moschen" – appeared on stage. Soon he was . . . manipulating glass balls. Manipulating as in the root of the word, using hands to move them, then using hands to make them look like they were moving by themselves. The balls looked like crystal Christmas tree ornaments and they seemed as if he couldn't drop them if he tried. They rolled around and under his arm and he exchanged them from one hand to the other – "It looks like he has six hands," I heard someone, maybe the mother behind us, say. The juggler was transfixed, looking so closely at what he was doing, as if that movement was all that mattered, and that would ever matter, and we were transfixed. "We" meaning two Baby Boomers without children. I couldn't speak for anyone else. After a while I felt the calm whoosh in my chest I get from art I really like –

Louis Sullivan's ornaments, certain early twentieth-century vases, all kinds of shrines. There were some less-than-sublime moments, too. There were goofy ones, such as when he got a volunteer from the audience and had him reach out to grab and bite an apple while Moschen juggled it, and some slow ones where the stage seemed just too dark, and the music, too, and I surprised myself with mid-afternoon sleepiness. The children in the audience had been generally quiet, and I suddenly thought, *Maybe they're all asleep.*

At intermission the man in front of us was saying, "At forty dollars a seat, leaving shouldn't be an option." The boy behind us said, "That was the second most boring thing I've ever seen." The most boring had involved Philip Glass music and, I think, images projected on a screen. My true love and I went to the lobby and waited for coffee. A woman in line in front of us was asking a cluster of children, "Do you want to stay or go to the Rainforest Cafe?" Kids were running in circles in the lobby, and when we got back to our seats, the extended family in front of us was much diminished. Apparently seven of them had exercised the option to leave.

It's too bad they cleared out because the second set was brighter and faster. Moschen twirled hoops so that they looked like wings, and for the finale, made circles of fire with lighted torches. Did you like the second half better? I asked the boy and girl behind me, a loaded question, of course, and they answered yes, and seemed like they meant it. A mother of a very small boy clambering over the steps from the lobby said he'd really liked the show, and she'd had to shush him so he wouldn't scream out, "Triangle!" "Circle!"

This is the real thing, I wanted to say to all the kids who hadn't appreciated Moschen in motion. He's doing this by himself, without smoke or mirrors or digitalization, he could do more or less the same thing in your backyard or the supermarket parking lot. I felt like some spectre from the twentieth century, advocating the old ways. Take away the lighting and some of the music, and this could be fifteen hundred years ago. (When was glass first blown?) Watch a man twirling torches – that could have be choreographed the mythical day after Prometheus stole fire from the gods and gave it to humans.

On New Year's Eve my true love and I took the creaky old subway to Buckingham Fountain for the fireworks. We brought percussive instruments from home. I clanged a butter knife against a metal candle holder and he used a *grager*, the metal rotary noisemaker used on Purim to drown out the name of the villain Haman. Inspired by that practice, we walked around the fountain, naming scourges of the millennium as best we could. Hitler, we said, then made noise, metal on metal. Stalin. The Black Plague. And we tried to remember exactly when the Dark Ages were, when Genghis Khan was alive and plundering. I hoped people wouldn't take us the wrong way and think we were neo-Nazis. (And no one would take us for observant Jews – if we were, we'd be at home or at the synagogue this Shabes night.)

Two nights later we had dinner at our friends Jack and Val's. Jack originated the slogan, back in the Berkeley Free Speech days, "Don't trust anybody over 30." He'll be sixty this spring. After dinner we played a game called Set, using a deck of cards with nothing but lozenge, diamond, or squiggly shapes on them. It was the kind of deck you could replicate in jail or in the Dark Ages or ancient Rome or anywhere there was paper and pigment or even leaves and a blade of some kind. Then we drove home into the future.

NOTES

EPIGRAPH

I'm grateful to Professor Allan Nadler of Drew University for leading me to this line, which had been echoing in my head – in English – for many years. The Yiddish is from *I Keep Recalling: The Holocaust Poems of Jacob Glatstein*, translated by Barnett Zumoff (Hoboken, NJ: Ktav, 1993). The translation is mine, affected by my memory of the line, and is not exactly the same as Zumoff's.

HOLOCAUST GIRLS/LEMON

Lvov sewer details and quote from *In the Sewers of Lvov: the Last Sanctuary from the Holocaust* by Robert Marshall (London: Collins, 1990). Borzykowski's comments from *Between Tumbling Walls* by Tuvia Borzykowski, translated from the Yiddish by Mendel Kohansky (Ghetto Fighters' House, Israel: Hakibbutz Hameuchad Publishing House, 1976).

SHEMA, THE FIRST PRAYER YOU LEARN

In Hebrew transliterations in this book, I use "ch" for the guttural. In Yiddish transliterations ("Getting to Yiddish," "The Ones You Break Bread With," "In the Mother Tongue" and others) I use mostly the standard YIVO spelling, and thus "kh" for the guttural.

KAVKA/40

Kafka biographical information from Ernst Pawel's *The Nightmare of Reason: A Life of Franz Kafka* (New York: Farrar, Straus, and Giroux, 1984). The Kafka quote in "Plain Scared" is from the same source. There is no Starbucks in Prague – at least not yet. The company said in March 2002 that it has no imminent plans to open cafés in the Czech Republic.

THE LANGUAGE OF *HEIMATLOS*

The most comprehensive, recent books on Gryszpan are Gerald Schwab's *The Day the Holocaust Began: The Odyssey of Herschel Grynszpan* (New York: Praeger, 1990) and *Kristallnacht: The Unleashing of the Holocaust* by Anthony

Read and David Fisher (New York: Peter Bedrick Books, 1989). Schwab paints a more sympathetic portrait. The man at the embassy gave me *L'Hôtel de Beauharnais: La résidence de l'Ambassadeur d'Allemagne à Paris* by Claus von Kameke (Stuttgart: Deutsche Verlags-Anstalt GmbH, 1968). Information on Schwartzbard and Frankfurter is from *Violent Justice: How Three Assassins Fought to Free Europe's Jews* (Amherst NY: Prometheus Books, 1994) by Felix and Myoko Imonti. The interview with Grynszpan's family appeared in the *Jerusalem Post International Edition*, week ending Nov. 12, 1998. I found that article and useful documents in the archives of the *Centre de Documentation Juive Contemporaine* in Paris. Jewish Brigade quote is by Johanan Peltz from *In Our Own Hands: The Hidden Story of the Jewish Brigade in World War II*, produced by Chuck Olin, Chuck Cooper, and Matthew Palm, directed by Chuck Olin, 85 min., Chuck Olin Associates, 1998, videocassette. The quote from the Krakow Jewish underground newspaper is from *The Cracow [Memorial] Book* (Jerusalem: Mosad HaRav Kook/Rav Kook Institute, 1959), edited by A. Bauminger and others. The German historian Hans-Juergen Doescher has recently claimed that he has found documents that do show that Herschel and vom Rath were lovers.

CHICAGO: LOSS OF PROPERTY

According to a U.S. Department of Justice 1998 study, "Criminal Victimization and Perceptions of Community Safety in 12 Cites" (including Chicago), "Annual findings from the NCVS [National Crime Victimization Survey] have indicated that most violent crimes across the Nation involve victims and offenders of the same race." In general, black urban residents are more likely than whites to experience violent crime, but in Chicago in 1998 slightly more whites than blacks reported being victims of violent crimes – over six percent compared to five percent. Nationally, and in Chicago as well, more black households than white reported they were victims of theft and robbery. I'd like to thank Bernardine Dohrn for leading me to this source.

YIZKOR, MEMORIAL SERVICE

Details about the funeral service from Joan Kruckewitt's *The Death of Ben Linder* (New York: Seven Stories Press, 1999). Kruckewitt reports that his family returned to Nicaragua for the inauguration of the Cuá-Bocay hydroelectric plant, Ben's second project. That ceremony was held on April 28, 1994, the seventh anniversary of Ben's death.

I spent the summer of 1989 in Managua teaching English. I visited Matagalpa with a friend, and we went to Ben Linder's grave there. Surrounded by crosses in the hilly cemetery, there's Ben's flat dark stone, with a unicycle carved into it.

AFTERWARDS

According to his synagogue, my grandfather's *Hebrew* name was Shalom Layb, though it sounds suspiciously like Yiddish. In Yiddish it would be Sholom Leyb. On the other side of the family, there's also a history of combining and confusing Yiddish and Hebrew names.

MONICA AND HANNAH

Sources include *Monica's Story* by Andrew Morton (New York: St. Martin's, 1999); *The Testing of Hanna Senesh* by Ruth Whitman, with a historical background by Livia Rothkirchen (Detroit: Wayne State, 1986); *Hannah Senesh: Her Life and Diary*, introduced by Abba Eban (New York: Schocken, 1972); *Blessed Is the Match: The Story of Jewish Resistance* by Marie Syrkin (Philadelphia: Jewish Publication Society, 1947); *The Summer That Bled: The Biography of Hannah Senesh* by Anthony Masters (New York: St. Martin's, 1972).

EATING HORSE

Information on Austria and Waldheim from *One, by One, by One: Facing the Holocaust* by Judith Miller (New York: Touchstone, 1990); *The Viennese: Splendor, Twilight, and Exile* by Paul Hofmann (New York: Doubleday, 1988); *Hitler and the Forgotten Nazis: A History of Austrian National Socialism* by Bruce F. Pauley (Chapel Hill: University of North Carolina, 1981); *Facts on File 1992*; and news reports: Reuters, July 26, 1987, and Aug. 2, 1988; *Time*, Feb. 29, 1988, and July 6, 1992; *The Washington Post*, March 13, 1988; UPI, July 26, 1988; *The New Republic*, Sept. 5, 1994. Post–World War I details, especially about eating horse, from Hofmann.

AMALEK

I discovered years later that the book I'd read in the Manhattan bookstore was David Roskies' *Against the Apocalypse: Responses to Catastrophe in Modern Jewish Culture* (Cambridge: Harvard, 1984).

Some of the pieces in this book were published in the following journals and magazines, sometimes in slightly different versions or with different titles, and are reprinted with grateful permission:

"Afterwards" ["The Long Goodbye"], *Chicago Reader* (June 6, 1997): 12–15.

"Amalek," *Sarajevo: An Anthology for Bosnian Relief*, ed. John Babbitt, Carolyn Feucht, and Andie Stabler (Elgin, IL: Elgin Community College, 1993), 307–9.

"Anne Franks in Texas," *Tikkun* 6 (Sept./Oct. 1991): 47–48.

"At the Rose of Sharon Spiritual Church," *West Side Stories*, ed. George Bailey (Chicago: City Stoop Press, 1992), 117–24.

"Chicago: Loss of Property," *Wigwag* (Apr. 1990): 29–52.

"Eating Horse," *Literal Latte* 6 (Mar./Apr. 2000): 14.

"Holocaust Girls/Lemon," *Ploughshares* 20 (fall 1994): 148–50.

"In the Mother Tongue" ["Di Vagina Monologuen"], *Chicago Reader* (Nov. 11, 2000): 8; "Adult-Ed Class Puzzles 'Vagina Monologues' in Mother Tongue," *Forward* (Dec. 15, 2000): 13–14; "If the 'Story' Could Talk . . . ," *In These Times* (Feb. 19, 2001): 38.

"Juggling: The New Year," ["Art for the Ages"] *Chicago Reader* (Jan. 7, 2000): 13.

"*Kavka*/40," *New Letters* 63 (spring 1997): 11–20. Reprinted with permission of *New Letters* and the Curators of the University of Missouri.

"Margot's Diary," *Creative Nonfiction* 10 (summer 1998): 23–26.

"Mexico on $15 a Day," *North American Review* 227 (Nov./Dec. 1992): 14.

"Monica and Hannah" ["A Tale of Two Women"], *Chicago Reader* (June 11, 1999): 18–20, 22–23.

"Plain Scared, Or: There Is No Such Thing as Negative Space, the Art Teacher Said," *Crab Orchard Review* 6 (spring/summer 2001): 211–15.

"Shema, the First Prayer You Learn," *Belles Lettres* 9 (winter 1993/94): 47–48.

"The Children of Theresienstadt," *Witness* 12 (spring 1998): 60–66.

"The Language of *Heimatlos*," *The New England Review* 21 (summer 2000): 113–26.

"The Ones You Break Bread With" [excerpt, "Tests of Faith"], *Chicago Reader* (Feb. 9, 2001): 12, 14–15.

"Vacation at Club Dead," *The Progressive* 51 (July 1987): 34.

"Yizkor (Memorial Service)," *Response* 57 (winter 1990): 39–43.